The God of Healing

The God of Healing

Michael Harold Brown

Spirit Daily Publishing
www.spiritdaily.com
11 Walter Place
Palm Coast, Florida 32164

The publisher recognizes and accepts that the final authority regarding the apparitions in the Catholic Church rests with the Holy See of Rome, to whose judgment we willingly submit.

—*The Publisher*

The God of Healing by Michael Harold Brown

Copyright © 2015 Michael H. Brown

Published by Spirit Daily Publishing

For additional copies, write:
Spirit Daily Publishing
11 Walter Place
Palm Coast, Florida 32164

or contact: www.spiritdaily.com

ISBN 978-0-692-54462-4

Printed in the United States of America   First Edition

*To Jesus Christ, Who heals today
as He did two thousand years ago*

1

Our Creator wants us whole

'I, the Lord, am your healer.' (Exodus 15:26)

There's no doubt whatsoever that God can heal anybody of anything. He is the "God of healing." We have to look no further than Jesus. It was healing—of epilepsy, of deafness, of many maladies—that until His death and Resurrection most defined Him as "miraculous."

In the New Testament Jesus was constantly going to or returning from a healing.

Think of what He did. Think of how quickly He did it. If it was God's Will, the healing was instantaneous. He even brought folks back from the dead.

Miracles of healing still occur—in fact, more than ever—as God pours Himself out to us in these dark days. There have been remarkable cases. I recall Barbara Smith, a dear and devout woman from the Marian Peace Center in Joy, Michigan. Barb told me the incredible story about how during a pilgrimage she'd slipped and fallen to the hard floor of a shower stall, feeling and actually hearing bones break and joints unhinge! It was terrifying—writhing on the cold floor, unable to move, but praying for help (as Barb always prayed). Suddenly, she said, there was the feeling of an angel, as some force lifted her back to her feet—literally—and her bones and joints snapped back together. The fractures, she said, were healed *instantly*.

Implausible? Yes. True? Knowing Barb as I did, I have no doubt.

God had put Barb back together, literally, implausibly, inexplicably!

Perhaps the most incredible healing on record, because it was so well documented, was one effected by the great Saint Padre Pio of San Giovanni Rotundo, Italy. It took place in February of 1949. Although the cures of many diseases, including cancer, are attributed by skeptics to "spontaneous remission," *this* was a case where a construction worker named Giovanni Savino who was hurt in a blast of dynamite had a left eye that was badly damaged and his right one all but totally destroyed—leaving a pulpy mess in the otherwise empty socket. Afterward, in the hospital, Savino sensed a presence, felt someone touch the right side of his face (though no one was there), and smelled an aroma of sanctity so well known around Padre Pio. According to Bernard Ruffin (a Protestant author who was initially skeptical of Padre Pio, but described it as something that "can be classed most unambiguously" as a miracle), "later that morning an ophthalmologist came to examine Savino's left eye. For the first time since the accident, his face was left unbandaged. To their amazement, the doctors found that his shattered face was fully healed and covered with new skin." When Savino insisted he now could see, the doctors told him this was "crazy" because one eye "isn't there anymore." But when the ophthalmologist examined him more closely, there was now an eye in the right socket. To repeat: this was an eye that had been jelly when doctors first examined him! "For the rest of his life, Savino was blind in his left eye, the one that had been damaged but not lost in the explosion," wrote Ruffin. "He maintained good vision, however, in the right eye, which apparently had materialized after its predecessor had been emulsified."

We thus note—in this documented medical marvel—that God can intervene in an unusual way and in the most extreme of circumstances. Never lose hope. I will cite other incredible examples. The point: when God wants us to be healthy, and live, He can and does heal anything. He is Spirit and the spirit forms, maintains, and directs the physical. When the spirit directs the body to do something, the body does what's directed.

Through the years I have been sent dozens of accounts documenting miraculous healings: folks cured of everything from allergies and diabetes to cancer. I once interviewed a doctor who was delivered from advanced prostate cancer at a site of Mary's apparitions in Venezuela. As this man, Dr. Vinicio Arrieta, who was educated at Harvard, director of the School of Medicine at the University of Zulia, and had founded a major hospital in Caracas, told me, he was at the site, known as Betania, which means "Bethany" (officially declared as "sacred ground" by the bishop in 1987) and praying during an all-night vigil about the advanced cancer (which had entered his spine and registered an antigen level of 100; the normal value is 0 to 10), when the healing occurred. "They had given me two years to live," he said. But Heaven—and the Blessed Mother—had other plans. At five a.m., after dozing off, it seems Dr. Arrieta awoke and pleaded with God to let him live for his two children, vowing to cast off his pride and pretensions if the prayer was answered. "We got up at six in the morning and we broke our fast, and we sang a little song to the Virgin," said Dr. Arrieta, who had received two prior treatments of chemotherapy. "At eight in the morning the solar phenomena began in which the sun lost its light—it was illuminated but it lost its light. [as at Fatima] The center part became green. It began to spin on the inside like there was a circle on the inside and then it began to come nearer to us.

Dr. Vinicio Paz, a specialist who made the original diagnosis, said there was "no scientific explanation" for the recovery. They did a biopsy that was also negative. The cancer had simply—vanished. An estimated five hundred to a thousand had been healed at this site by the time of my interview back in the 1990s! The bishop, a psychologist, investigated events for himself and told me he had no doubt about it.

When an esteemed doctor documents his own cure (from something incurable), backed up by a bishop, with no chance of misdiagnosis, or spontaneous remission, I am certainly prone to believe. Actually, as we will see, there is no such *thing* as "incurable": God works where He so wills, and will do so till the end of time.

In our own era, miracles are countless.

The Creator wants us whole. He wants us healthy. He wants us happy. But life is a place of testing and evil, and we're tested hard. The toughest test may be illness. There are many causes for disease, some of which are from darkness, some from natural sources (allowed because they help work out our salvation); others are sacrifice. We say "redemptive": In ways that are mysterious, suffering can purify the soul, making it better suited for Heaven. When we suffer, we often grow closer to Jesus. We purge. A serious illness brings us to dependence and dependence to humility. When we're suffering, our hearts are more open to love. We're more compassionate. We're more humble. It divorces us from worldliness. In the wake of a diagnosis, things that once seemed so important (and urgent, "in the world")—bank accounts, homes, jobs—suddenly are less so (if they maintain their importance at all). Illness clarifies. It brings us back to the child within (and Jesus taught that we will not see Heaven unless we are innocent). It simplifies. It clears the eyesight. It brings us not only to more prayer, but prayer from the heart.

I have known many with serious illnesses who through the illness gained a brilliant understanding of God (and even in suffering glow with love for Him). Recently, I met an elderly man who survived one of the very most serious of operations: surgery for cancer of the esophagus. This entails not only a tremendously large surgical opening on the front of the body, but a second huge surgery on the back, and even then, if not during the operation, the patient often dies soon after. But quite a warrior, this fellow not only survived but thrived, filled with faith; when I saw him last he was beaming, radiant, and told me he still serves each day as a Eucharistic minister and leads a weekly praise group!

His "flask" had been made new for choice wine after desperate illness.

Does God heal all those who are so loyal?

I know very holy people who've succumbed to ailments. When it's our time, it's our time. But He *does* heal. There is the case of Jeff Markin: On October 20, 2006, the 53-year-old mechanic, soaked with sweat, stumbled into the emergency room at Palm Beach Gardens Hospital in Florida, suffering from acute anxiety and an upset stomach. Shortly after, Markin collapsed into a heap from a massive heart attack. When a cardiologist named Dr. Chauncey W. Crandall was summoned, Markin was barely clinging to life; in Dr. Chauncey's words, the emergency room was a "war zone." Two IV lines had been thrust into the mechanic, along with a ventilator and stomach tube.

Already Jeff had been hit six times with electrical paddles, shocks so intense his body leapt above the stretcher. They "called the code" on him. The conclusion was unavoidable: Jeff Markin was dead. His time of passing was declared at 8:05 a.m. Dr. Crandall and a nurse who was charged with preparing the body for the morgue remained behind. "The doctors and nurses had been working on the patient for nearly forty minutes," wrote Dr. Crandall in a book, *Raising the Dead: A Doctor Encounters the Miraculous.* "I noticed that his head, especially his lips, and his fingers and toes were cyanotic—black with death from lack of oxygen. When cyanosis appears, there's little hope." Tubes were removed and IVs taken from Markin's arms. "With my report complete, I headed toward the door and back to my runway of patients," recounted Dr. Crandall, who was educated at Yale. "Before I crossed its threshold, however, I sensed God was telling me to turn around and pray for that man. This seemed foolish—an idle thought caused by the stress of the situation or even mischievous influence. But then [there was a] sense of God telling me this occurred a second time and more forcefully. I did not know this man, and, frankly, I felt embarrassed by the impulse to pray for him. But I knew that when I had ignored such impulses in the past I never felt peace afterward. I stood by the body, and although the words I said came through me, I had no sense of devising them. It was more as if I were God's intercom, relaying a 'divine code.'"

Dr. Crandall began to pray next to the body: "Father God, I cry out for this man's soul," he said. "If he does not know You as his Lord and Savior, raise him from the dead now, in Jesus' Name." The nurse looked up at him as if he'd lost his mind. Crandall didn't care. His arm shot up as if by its own accord in a gesture of prayer and praise as if to catch a gift from above. At that moment another doctor walked back in and Dr. Crandall asked him to administer one last shock to Markin.

"Dr. Crandall," said the other doctor in disbelief, "I can't shock the patient one more time. I've shocked him again and again. He's dead."

Crandall insisted and after the next shock, a heartbeat returned—a *regular* one. No halting; no skips. Markin's blackened fingers twitched. Soon, the "corpse" was mumbling. It was something they'd never witnessed before. The nurse released "a long, piercing wail right out of the movies," recalled Dr. Crandall. Markin's pulse was normal. A perfect *heartbeat*! His abdomen fluttered: he was breathing on his own.

Case closed. A miracle. *Markin's skin had blackened.* Cyanosis. It was partly dead. Suddenly, it was viable flesh. From a place of darkness (which is what Markin saw while unconscious), he came back to life and Light.

"I make all things new," said the Lord in *Revelation* (21:5).

When God wants to bring us back, and when others are praying—when we have cleared darkness—wonders result.

Markin's daughter had been in the parking lot, praying both for a medical miracle and her father's conversion.

Immediately upon resuscitation, Markin accepted Jesus.

2

God is in total control

'It will be well with you and your days shall be multiplied and prolonged as the days of Heaven upon the earth' (Deuteronomy 11:9, 21).

The Lord works mysteriously, more so with healing than anything.

There's a key word here: darkness. That means sin. It entails a lack of belief. It means an attachment to the ways of the world.

Most of all, darkness means *spirits* of darkness. We'll discuss this.

For when we detach from that—from the world, from luxuries, from lust, from what the baptismal rite calls "glamour of evil," when we forsake materialism and correct a lack of love (selfishness)—we stand a chance of healing no matter what shape we're in.

One of the definitions of heal is to "purify or bring from darkness."

When I say we stand a chance of healing "no matter what," let me cite the case of Dr. George Rodonaia, himself a physician who was brought back from death after a "fatal" car accident in Moscow, reviving when a coroner began to cut him open in the morgue! He'd been "dead" for days. He too found himself in a place of darkness. Yet through the mercy of God, Dr. Rodonaia also recovered (and became a minister in Texas). I once spoke to a former television reporter, Ranelle Wallace of Glendora, California, who was in a horrible small-plane crash, her craft hitting the side of a mountain and super-hot jet fuel exploding all around, deeply charring more than three-quarters of her body. Almost immediately her flesh had begun falling off in clumps, and if that wasn't enough, she gashed and bruised herself severely as she struggled to find help on remote terrain in central Utah (before finally succumbing to unconsciousness and "death"). While "on the other side," Ranelle saw the nature of her physical existence and that it wasn't her time yet. The desperately wounded woman said she found herself in a light that was "like a nuclear explosion; the light pierced me. Every particle of me was shot through with blinding, brilliant light, and I had a feeling of transparency. My skin didn't burn. My eyes still saw. I floated in this light, bathed in it, and the love that surrounded me and filled me was sweeter and finer than anything I had ever felt. I was changed by it, refined, rarefied, made pure. I basked in its sweetness, and the traumas of the past were far behind me, forgotten, and transformed by peace." She lived (and rehabilitated) despite fantastic odds.

There is the physical that is a shadow of a perfect, indestructible, and unblemished heavenly version. "If there is a natural body, there is also a spiritual body," said Paul (*1 Corinthians* 15:44-46). "Just as we have borne the image of the earthy, we will also bear the image of the heavenly" (15:48). Brain tumors, leukemia, or simple afflictions like allergies can have a spiritual basis and thus are often *healed* spiritually. What is in Heaven shapes what is on earth.

In Rwanda, Africa, three Catholic schoolgirls (at a Church-approved site of apparitions called Kibeho) were taken by the Blessed Mother on "journeys" to Heaven, hell, and purgatory and during those journeys their bodies registered impossibly low breathing, blood pressure, and heart rates—or none at all—when medical personnel examined them. Like Markin, one girl showed signs of *rigor mortis*. Yet all three awoke fully intact at the end of their "trips." They had returned from the dead (the last after three days of virtually no signs of life, her return on Easter Sunday!).

If God can raise Lazarus He can raise you and He can certainly heal your sinuses! Let's recount: in *John* 11:39-43, Jesus finds Lazarus in a tomb, telling those with Him to open it. "Martha, the dead man's sister, said to Him, 'Lord, by now there will be a stench; he has been dead for four days.' Jesus said to her, 'Did I not tell you that if you believe you will see the glory of God?' So they took away the stone. And Jesus raised His eyes and said, *'Father, I thank you for hearing Me. I know that you always hear Me; but because of the crowd here I have said this, that they may believe that you sent Me.'* And when He had said this, He cried out in a loud voice, *'Lazarus, come out!'* The dead man came out, tied hand and foot with burial bands, and his face was wrapped in a cloth."

God is all-powerful with total control over the physical and often when we think it was a doctor or surgeon who came to the rescue was angels doing His bidding. "I remember standing about ten feet up and ten feet to the side of my body on the [operating] table," said a man named Jonathan who had a near-death experience during critical surgery. "A person was standing next to me, but I didn't look at him/her. I had no fear or questions to ask; I just observed. Around the table were at least a dozen nurses and doctors. But what was so emotional was the presence of [glowing] people that I can only describe as angels. Each angel was guiding the hands of the staff they were standing next to. I heard no noise, no voices, no music. It was peacefully quiet. I don't remember details too specific, such as what tools were used or the exact position of my body, but only because I was focused so much on the angels guiding the staff in everything they did, from walking to the use of the tools within my chest cavity. Even after the operation, I still had an unusual peace and no fear. The doctor said it was the best operation he had ever gone through—there were no problems at all—and he was impressed by my rate of recovery."

My point: when you tap into that—when you ask God, in the Name of Jesus, to send healing angels, when you thank Him in advance, as did Jesus, when you are in touch with your spiritual side—a wondrous recovery can happen. As Dr. Crandall said, a prayer for help is like a laser that reaches Heaven.

In Dr. Crandall's case, it was just a quick and not even especially heartfelt prayer. The important thing: he did what he was told. He moved the mountain. Obedience.

Nothing is impossible, once He intervenes.

3

Invisible forces

'I will remove sickness from your midst' (Exodus 23:25)

That there are invisible forces at work controlling our anatomies and their intricate functions should be obvious by exactly this feature: how elaborate and ingeniously complex the body is fashioned. God is astounding! This could never have occurred by chance! A human eye alone is far too complex for anyone to explain as a product of random gene mutations (what they call "natural selection"); in fact, even a single cell is too complex for happenstance. How is it that skin knows how to repair a wound and with such precision that the scratch, insect bite, burn, or cut (unless it's too large) doesn't leave a scar? How does the body know to provoke swelling or cause the skin to peel in order to expel a sliver? Or to cause a fever to kill bacteria? *How could simple physical forces, left on their own, know to do that?*

They can't. These and countless other functions are orchestrated by a spiritual dimension that oversees, organizes, and adjusts our physiology. Did you ever consider how many functions the liver alone carries out and how often it takes up doing something if another organ that usually does this is not properly functioning? It stores. It digests. It metabolizes. It produces. It detoxifies. Or take blood vessels:

when new ones grow to replace blocked ones, is this marvelous repair sheer luck? There are also "homeostatic" processes in the body which know how to emanate perspiration when the body gets too hot or form "gooseflesh" when our skin is cold or to provoke an itch that causes us to scratch and by doing so draw healing blood cells to an area.

Look at the symmetry between the right and left sides of your body. There is no "evolutionary" reason for such perfection, and no way that random mutations alone could be responsible for *any* (let alone all) the symmetry in nature. A bird's perfectly shaped, colored, and aligned feathers are not fortuitous. They were designed this way! Look at the complex changes in a woman's body when she is pregnant and the incredible miracle of birth: just something nature conjured up dumbly? The immune system of a human can recognize tens of thousands of agents that may harm and dispense with them; it's so complicated we are still only beginning to log its many interactions; it knows how to create and build up white blood cells if there is an infection. It can nullify thousands of microbes!

God did all that—the same God Who can heal your body when it's an ill body and sculpt it into healthfulness. If it's time to call you home, He calls you home: No amount of prayer will forestall it. He does what is best for your *eternity*. We're not meant to live on earth forever.

But the spirit and body work together, and when there is balance, when there is harmony, when we are still performing a mission He has assigned to us, there is health and (even if there is suffering) contentment.

We are temples of the Holy Spirit, and we find health when we are in harmony with that Spirit. It thus behooves us to take care of that temple! Neglect of health indicates a soul that lacks maturity. When we enfold ourselves with His

Power, we're secure; there's a buffer; the way is open to health (again, be it His Will). Too often, when we're ill, what greets us is the cold sterile atmosphere of a doctor's office. Our medical system is far too oriented to numbers, money, and a worldview that's solely physical. Look at the very name for modern healing: "practicing medicine." It is entirely based on physical cures, neglecting the spiritual component (and thus closing off many chances for success).

Physical healing must be accompanied by spiritual input.

Years ago I spoke to Dr. Michael Torosian (a surgeon) and Veruschka R. Biddle (a psychotherapist), both determined to spread the word about the importance of "spiritual healing." They wrote a book together. Trained to help people with traumas, Dr. Biddle takes on patients who are ready to give up—who in some cases have begun preparing for their funerals—and seeks to turn all that around, knowing that with Christ, all things are possible. What it takes is a connection to God and abandonment to Him. With that comes "an incredible spiritual transformation that gives them peace," said Dr. Biddle. "Suddenly they become very calm and peaceful. The peace is quite mysterious, and they are placed in a position of new power." Underline the word "surrender." With God, there is a way out of every situation, even those that seem to have no exit. Our Blessed Mother said, *"I am your mother full of goodness and Jesus is your great Friend. Do not fear anything in His Presence. Give Him your heart, from the bottom of your heart. Tell Him your sufferings; thus will you be invigorated in prayer, with a free heart, in a peace without fear. It is up to you to pray and I will take care of the rest. You cannot even imagine how powerful God is. Pray and fast. You need enthusiasm in your prayer. May you pray in meditation for a long time and fervently. I invite you to say these words: 'I love God in everything.' With love, one obtains everything."*

It's not just words: there is never the need for despair. I have seen plenty of people go years or decades beyond the prognosis—decades. We're *all* terminal. And also we all live forever. Does that mean everyone who prays and has faith will receive a miracle? As I have said, how God responds is up to Him. We can never predict it! What we need to know is that everything that happens to us and is ordained by God (as opposed to caused by sin) is for eternal betterment. "The focus is to become more Christ-like, and *trust* is a major, major issue," Biddle said. "Everything goes so smoothly when we pray. If you do not trust, you live in fear. A lot of people forget that they have a personal guardian with them all the time, and when you're in a situation of illness or fright or loss and you know that there's a spiritual companion as well as God, it gives you that extra security. When you have trust, something beautiful happens." In their book Dr. Biddle recounts entering the room of a 45-year-old woman named Lynn who was nearing the end of a struggle with cancer. "I was suddenly overcome with a deep sense of a Divine Presence in Lynn's room," recalled the psychotherapist. "The room was filled with such peace and love that I was moved to tears. As I approached Lynn's bed I suddenly sensed the presence of two large, beautiful angels standing on either side of her bed. The angels were placing their arms gently underneath Lynn's very frail body, just as though they were ready to lift her up. I was in such awe of this image that I was not sure how to tell Lynn or her family what I was experiencing. I wondered if I was seeing a vision or if I was creating a picture in my own mind. I did not want to question what I was experiencing, it was just too beautiful."

According to Dr. Kenneth Ring, an expert in death experiences, one man who nearly succumbed to leukemia (but was miraculously healed) testified that he saw Jesus with eyes like "shooting fire" and heard the words, *"That's enough, it's dead, it's gone"* (in relation to his illness). Another (granting us a glimpse into how healing is actually conducted) saw "an entity in a colored cloak of indescribably beautiful colors, and a brightness most intense. This something stood at the right-hand side of my head; two hands were lightly placed on my body and slowly moved down to my feet, and up the left side, pausing at my head, and then was gone. I have no recollection of anything until the next day. From then I made a very rapid recovery and was soon back with my family."

Light brings life.

We're never without hope because we are never alone. "I remember one girl who had her wisdom teeth out and had an allergic reaction to the anesthesia," said Dr. Biddle. "When she woke up after three days in a coma, she asked her mother, 'Who is Philip?' Her mother turned white and asked why. The girl said, 'Because I saw Philip in Heaven and he told me I needed to go back and he even looks like me.' Then her mother said, 'He was your twin brother who was lost. We actually had had a Christian burial and named him Philip.' They had never told her about it."

Know that the bottom line, again, is that you *live forever.* Don't accept an evil report—when the devil attempts to discourage (and define) you. You won't be victorious if you despair, if you plan for defeat.

Let's talk more about the "evil report":

In 1958, Saint Padre Pio to use his example again was afflicted by bronchial pneumonia—prostrated by it. Terribly. It wouldn't leave despite doctors' best efforts. Early in May they called it "pleurisy" and ordered absolute bed rest, but nothing worked. "After May 5, he was confined to his room, unable to celebrate Mass or hear Confessions," recounts Ruffin. "Three times during May, Pio's physicians drew more than a quart of bloody fluid from his pleural cavities without bringing relief. Padre Carmelo of Sessano, the guardian, summoned well-known specialists. After making various tests, they arrived at a grim diagnosis: 'pleural neoplasm with bloody exudations.' That's cancer. They recommended a terrible regimen of chemotherapy. With solemn faces, three doctors entered Pio's room and told him that he had cancer and had no more than a few months to live.

"To their shock, [Padre Pio] burst out laughing and told them they did not know what they were talking about"!

He refused their "evil report." He also refused chemotherapy. In August, on the Feast of Our Lady of the Snows, a famous pilgrim statue from Fatima was brought by helicopter to that barren part of Italy where Pio lived and for several days faithfully prayed. It was also brought to the church at his monastery—where, despite the illness, Saint Pio had aides carry him to the sanctuary and he managed to kneel before the Madonna, draping a golden rosary around her.

Afterward, Padre Pio, breathless and in pain, was carried back to bed. "When the statue was being conveyed away by helicopter, Pio murmured, 'Dear Mother, ever since you came to Italy, I have been immobilized by sickness. Now that you're leaving, aren't you going to say even a word to me?'" wrote Ruffin. "In the twinkling of an eye, the padre felt 'a mysterious force' surge through his body. Immediately he shouted, 'I'm healed!' and leaped from his bed. Pio felt completely cured. Within two weeks he had resumed all his duties."

Padre Pio had not limited God. He had not "programmed" death. He did not accept the report. (Also, he had honored His mother.) Do you believe in the New Testament? "Approximately one-third of the Gospel is taken up by the cures wrought by Jesus in the brief period of His public life," noted Father Raniero Cantalamessa, the preacher of the Pontifical Household in Rome (the one who preaches to popes). "It is impossible to eliminate these miracles, or to give them a natural explanation, without distorting the whole Gospel and making it incomprehensible."

Many miracles are gradual or subtle. Not all are Lazaruses. Bishop M. Pearse Lacey of Toronto once told me about a skin wound from a cancer operation on his shoulder that closed in a remarkable way during a trip to Betania. "I had been operated on and a cancer removed but for some strange reason the hole wouldn't heal, so I was experiencing the need of three to four changes of bandages a day," said Bishop Lacey. "I'd been to Lourdes four times, I'd been to Medjugorje (in Bosnia-Hercegovina), I'd been to Fatima twice. There's been this yearning, this desire, over the years, to grow closer to Mary because I realized that it manifests a desire to come closer to the Lord; I knew that Mary would be the great medium for this. That was my intention in going to Betania, but naturally I was very conscious of the cancer operation and the lack of cure in it." The bishop put blessed water on his wound and paid a personal visit to the seer, Maria Esperanza. "She prayed over me for about ten minutes," Bishop Lacey told me. "In any case, within a matter of a day the shoulder draining just dried up completely and I never went back to bandaging it again."

Maria herself had a long history of suffering and illness, especially as a girl. "It was my heart," she said. "I would have been fourteen or fifteen years old, and it was so painful. My heart was weakening. I had a heart condition, about one hundred and fifty beats a minute, which would make me faint, and they would have to take me to the hospital, where they gave me treatments. I couldn't breathe. It was an incredible agony. On November 8 in 1947, that was when I really got bad. I couldn't get up for three months. The doctors didn't know what to do. Some said one thing, others said another. They didn't really know what I had. It would seem like I was getting better and then I would get bad again. It was such a struggle. How I suffered! And I was getting thinner. My mother suffered so much. All my family thought I was going to die. Later they found a serious infection. Oh, I had terrible pains in my bones. I didn't eat anything. Just horrible pains. And so when I saw that I was dying, they brought me the Eucharist. My whole left side was paralyzed—my eye, my leg. I couldn't see out of my left eye. It was just incredible, the whole situation. I knew that life was leaving me, and I didn't know what to do.

"At that moment something happened, which I know for the world is impossible to believe. It's something very strange. I realized that the Lord lives among all of us, that He depends on each of our gestures, each of our actions—each one of us. He depends on our health and our lives, on our hopes, our dreams. He depends on our sickness, and He waits for us to look at Him. His eyes—how they penetrate! It's like radar the way He penetrates you with His eyes. I felt such heat entering me. I felt a vapor, or something like that. Very, very incredible. All of a sudden I sat up. I just felt the strength. And all of a sudden everything moved and the clock fell to the floor. My mother said, 'Earthquake! Earthquake!' She came running. They thought I was dying, and the whole building was reverberating, and everything was just making noise, and then in that moment I just sat up with such strength. I wrote something down. I don't know how I did that. The message said, *'Maria Esperanza, My mother and I will heal you. Do not become desperate. You will have peace and relief from your sickness. My Father has heard you and He will lift you up.'"* From there she went on to improvement—over a period—and total health.

Maybe it's a mystery, but that healing occurs is beyond question.

How far is our society, and sometimes our Church, going to go in denying this?

There are cases like Francis Pascal from Beaucaire in France, the second child to be healed (in a way that science would accept, at any rate) at the famous site of Lourdes, that were not so gradual. He'd developed meningitis at the tender age of three, leaving him blind and without use of his limbs. In 1938 he was bathed in the water at the site, and suddenly was describing things he could *see*. This was an immediate cure, one doctors certified. He pointed a finger at a tricycle on the nearby esplanade. He also regained use of his limbs! In 1946 the Medical Bureau of Verifications at Lourdes examined him and confirmed that it "maintained for more than eight years, for which no medical explanation was possible." He spent the rest of his life at his great joy: reading classical novels.

A religious named Sister Marguerite had been afflicted with edema, renal disease, and angina. As her condition worsened, those taking care of her decided to replace her medications with water from Lourdes and at the same time her fellow sisters initiated a nine-day novena to Our Lady.

On the last day of the novena, Sister Marguerite's pain began to disappear, and she made a complete recovery. A day later she was back to performing her regular tasks at the convent.

When a wound closes suddenly, the day before a scheduled amputation, following deep prayer, you know something is up; this occurred in another case in Bosnia-Hercegovina.

4

The radiance of Heaven

'I am the health of your countenance and your God' (Psalms 43:5)

The deeper we pray the more we can focus on every part of the body and ask the Holy Spirit to protect and heal our brains, ears, necks, lymph glands, throats (call on Saint Blaise), blood vessels, hearts, lungs (Saint Bernardine), eyes (Saint Lucy), stomachs, intestines, colons, reproductive organs, breasts (Saint Agatha), joints, and skin. Throughout life, our cells, tissues, and organs take a beating from the environment, bad nutrition, along with simple age, and so it is wise to go through one's life and pray to rectify potential health problems.

God is the Great Physician and each cell comes from the life force of His Spirit. That Force, as we have seen, can heal anyone of anything. One must cooperate by casting away resentment, unforgiveness, and anger, which also wear on our organs, and so start a journey to health by going through a review of life and loving anyone we have not loved and forgiving everyone we have not forgiven. Pray. Meditate on Scripture. Listen. Ask Jesus to "reverse the clock." Let's say you smoked: go back, ask the Lord to forgive you for smoking, cast out spirits that may be associated with nicotine, and ask Him to pervade your lungs and heal them. "Soak" yourself in holiness. Cast out spirits of "tobacco" and "addiction." When you're clean inside, entities are not comfortable; Jesus called them "unclean spirits"; foul does not mesh with clean. The Lord will guide you. Your angels are there. Saint Raphael will come. (Stomach? Saint Charles Borromeo.) If you drank too much, focus on your liver. If you ate the wrong things, focus on your colon (and stomach), if obese, cast out the spirit of gluttony. If there is a genetic weakness, ask the Lord to reconfigure your genes. Do a life review of your health and pray over each organ, looking for blotches that may cause future problems, *for the non-physical* transmits to the physical and it is Grace that heals through deliverance. If you have jealousy, this could produce bile (bitterness). If you're angry, you harden your heart (and its vessels; "Harden not your heart," *Psalm* 95:8). If you reject yourself, you may have acne. If your heart oozes "gall," go back through your life and neutralize this acid. (An acidic system is more prone to cancer.) If you've failed to forgive, you may be attached in a "sick way" to whomever you have not forgiven.

It is often the spiritual garbage inside of us that attracts the "flies" that can carry disease and fester within (spreading "larvae"). More on this, too, shortly.

But first let's understand that our cells, tissues, and organs, working in miraculous concert, with astonishing complexity, are pervaded and vivified by spirit. As I said, there is a spiritual body that orchestrates anatomy and is empowered by the Holy Spirit. This is the light people see around those who are holy, especially Our Blessed Mother, the "halo" artists depict around saints. At Fatima, Mary was described as "radiating a light more clear and intense than a crystal glass filled with sparkling water when the rays of the burning sun shine through it," a light that "surrounded her, or rather, radiated from her," as there is also a light in and around every person who has allowed the Light of God to flourish and who has remained connected to the Source of life, a branch in the vineyard of Jesus. *Ecclesiastes*: "I am like a vine putting out graceful shoots, my blossoms are sweeter than honey." (Honey nourishes the body; it kills bacteria).

Teresa of Avila said (about the Light that gives us life) "it is not a radiance which dazzles, but a soft whiteness and an infused radiance which, without wearying the eyes, causes them the greatest delight; nor are they wearied by the brightness which they are seeing in this Divine beauty.

"So different from any earthly light is the brightness and light now revealed to the eyes that, by comparison with it, the brightness of our sun seems quite dim and we should never want to open our eyes again for the purpose of seeing it. It is as if we were to look at a very clear stream, in a bed of crystal, reflecting the sun's rays."

It's when we allow that light to dim or blur that trouble and breakdown begin. That shows the importance of praying to rid yourself of the devil's "hiss": obsession, oppression, depression, tension, duress, and stress (hear the snake?)—casting these out by *name* ("spirit of tension," "spirit of stress") and doing so in the Name of Jesus until you actually feel that the tension or oppression or discouragement leave. Evil comes with profanity, lust, hatefulness, unforgiveness, sloth, idleness, jealousy, resentment, the occult, violent reading material, and anything sinful—all spirits. Venial sins can be like flies gathering on a "window"—obscuring vision and entering (when a window is cracked). Note what Jesus told His disciples (*Matthew* 10:7-8): *"As you go, make this proclamation: 'The Kingdom of Heaven is at hand.' Cure the sick, raise the dead, cleanse the lepers, drive out demons."* In the Bible are twenty-five verses to do with the Lord casting out demonic or unclean spirits. When a demon was cast out, the mute could speak

(*Mark* 11:14); a person bent over could stand straight (*Luke* 13:10-16). Was it not a spiritual "something" that "seized" a man's son (*Matthew* 17:14) and caused epileptic fits? "He cast out the spirits with a word, and healed all who were ill," says *Matthew* (8:16). *"Behold, I cast out demons and perform cures,"* Our Lord said in *Luke* 13:32. We know that Jesus "rebuked the fever" and dispelled it. (Thus, a "spirit of feverishness.") We also know He forgave the paralytic his sins before He healed him.

God is the Great Physician. In deep quiet listen for Him. He reverses the curse; He reverses the letters in "evil" and turns them back into "live."

5

Mysterious causes?

'Who pardons all your iniquities, Who heals all your diseases'
(Psalms 103:3)

The Lord heals by His Word and so we must *meditate* on His Word, particularly passages that deal with healing. "Then they cried to the Lord in their trouble, and He saved them from their distress. He sent forth His word and healed them" (*Psalm* 107:19-20). "Praise the Lord, oh my soul, and forget not all His benefits—Who forgives all your sins and heals all your diseases" (*Psalm* 103:2-3). "Oh Lord my God, I called to you for help and you healed me" (*Psalm* 30:2). Remember that "Jesus went through all the towns and villages, teaching in their synagogues, preaching the good news of the kingdom, and healing every disease and sickness" (*Matthew* 9:35).

Everyone!

Luke the evangelist is thought to have been a physician. So we think: "Physician, heal thyself" (*Luke* 4:23).

That's hardly to say that all tumors are a chastisement or spiritual (though every ailment has some kind of spiritual implication). The wind blows where it may (*John* 3:8); there are natural causes. No one lives forever. It is wrong to be obsessed with longevity (our focus should be on Heaven). Human bodies are programmed for a limited time on earth and during that time we must nail the flesh to His Cross and crucify what is counter to eternity. In many cases we see the benefit of illness, which, as I said, may sanctify in the same way that the Lord sanctified cities. "Therefore behold, the days are coming," declared the Lord "when I will send to him those who tip vessels, and they will tip him over, and they will empty his vessels and shatter his jars" (*Jeremiah* 48:12). It can be a reordering: illness may be used to advance the soul.

But frequently it happens that darkness in spirit translates into physical darkness, often through the unseen shadows: a physical malady, sometimes across generations. Illness crosses generations. We curse ourselves through wrong thinking. Words can cast out a spirit or invite one. "It makes me sick," many say. "What a pain in the neck." (For all we know, this could lead to neck, head, or other ailments.) When we "stiffen our necks," are we prone to arthritis? If we're "fed up," or something is eating away at us, might we invite digestive distress? We say, "This is killing me." Do you think setting such a pattern of thought is wise, when we know that the mind can affect the body? Words and thoughts are powerful and with them we curse or bless ourselves. "The subconscious mind acts out on the body the unexpressed areas of conflict, either consciously, verbally, or physically, by selecting a target or end organ which can deal with them most appropriately," claimed a Christian psychiatrist from Oxford named Dr. Kenneth McAll (in *Healing the Family Tree*). "Every thought has a physical outlet. Feelings and thoughts have repercussions. The marked frequency of multiple sclerosis, anklylosing spondylitis, and ulcerative colitis in some families suggests a common denominator of unknown origin. In the arthritic and rheumatic, spasm and the consequent stagnation of an area may be caused by anger and resentment. If this is replaced by forgiveness and confidence, suddenly the central controlling impulses are released into normal balanced functioning."

A person "hunched over" with spondylitis may be "carrying" family burdens (for our discernment). In multiple sclerosis, posited the doctor, it could be nerves exposed to wounds in the immediate family, or past generations. Dr. McAll believed one common factor was a backlash of bitterness over traumatic family relationships. "A middle-aged woman in a wheelchair had been very angry with God ever since her only two pregnancies had miscarried," continued McAll (who was an associate with the Royal College of Psychiatrists). "In a church Eucharistic service, she apologized for her anger and prayed for the two children. Suddenly, a hot glow penetrated her whole being, she rose to her feet, and then walked all the way home."

In the Old Testament, evil was blamed for boils, tumors, and scabs "with an itch from which you cannot be healed" (*Deuteronomy* 28:27).

Wrote Dr. Crandall, whose own son had a malignant disease: "I'm convinced that cancer is not only a disease but a purposeful evil. Cancer is evil; just because you can't see malignant cells under a microscope doesn't mean they aren't an expression of Satan's will to destroy God's Creation. Satan comes to kill, steal, and destroy. Cancer is a demonic spirit; like so many things that reflect Satan's true character, cancer takes a good thing—cell reproduction— and introduces subtle twists that make it destructive, in fact, a killing machine . . . [He] had terrible nightmares and he claimed to see evil presences—wolves and demons. We thought he was only afraid of the dark and the unknown like any other child. But now that I've met other people who have a heightened sense of the spiritual world all around us, I'm not so sure. Just as I'm convinced that demons are real now, I'm convinced that there are people who get a glimpse of them now and again. I don't mean to be spooky or kooky. But there are more things in Heaven and earth than are realized in the way most of us look at life."

Spiritual elements interweave with the physical on a constant basis.

In some cases, cancer may come as a suffering that matures us; it may be there to offer up for society; it may be the nailing to the Cross. In this way, it's a positive, if suffered well (in union with Jesus). In other cases it may originate in anger, unforgiveness, or other malicious feelings (as Dr. McAll indicated), which is another reason to purge those emotions. If an illness is something that repeats down a family line, we should cast the spirit out with specificity ("spirit of allergy," "spirit of asthma," "spirit of pneumonia"—a word derived from the Greek *pneuma* for "wind," "spirit," or "breath"). Dr. McAll logged cases where "naming names" caused many types of illness (including a malignant tumors) to leave with a purging of negative emotions. "Becoming a pure instrument as a channel of God's Grace carries with it the gift of a new power," wrote Dr. McAll. "We choose to switch our thoughts to become a candle of the Lord, so that our prayers may rise like incense and change situations in the troubled world around us. Fear, pain, and disease are earthly; peace, love, and joy are everlasting."

6

Speak health into yourself

'It will be healing to your body And refreshment to your bones'
(Proverbs 3:8)

Meditate on the Bible. His Word heals; ours tend not to. Pray, read Scripture, and listen for His soft Voice, which is often a thought in the quiet of intuition. Fast. With fasting, said Mary, you can *"suspend the laws of nature,"* including laws that cause disease. Fasting expels evil.

Is there a curse hidden behind your ailment?

Whenever you are jealous—wishing someone less than the best, which is what jealousy is—you are leveling a curse, and curses boomerang. So does gossip, which removes Grace. "In the same way the tongue is a small member and yet has great pretensions," says the passage from *James* (3:5). "Consider how small a fire can set a huge forest ablaze. The tongue is also a fire. It exists among our members as a world of malice, defiling the whole body and setting the entire course of our lives on fire, itself set on fire by Gehenna."

Thus, forsake the negative and speak *health* into yourself.

Avoid fire, eat right, and you avoid inflammation.

Inflammation can be involved in everything from sciatica to Alzheimer's.

Like Abraham, put all on the altar of sacrifice.

One woman who had serious, "terminal" cancer placed signs all over her house that quoted uplifting passages from the Bible on miracles; she was healed and testifies nationally about it.

Perfection—everything falling exactly into place—is only in Heaven. Earth is a test. The Lord responds to the positive, and reacts to surrender. ("Lord, let Your Will be done, not mine"). When we're positive we're exhibiting faith. The negative drains light from your spirit. Look at every issue as a test for salvation.

Embrace the challenge.

Do that and you're speaking health into yourself.

A woman named Shirley Williams told the Christian Broadcast Network that she had been diagnosed with stage-four cancer—tumors that had metastasized into her lymph nodes, organs, and bones. Her doctor gave her ninety days to live. Her husband Mark wasn't buying it—and fled to the Bible for encouragement. He said, "Shirley, whose report are you going to believe? God's Word says that we shall live and not die and Shirley, it also says that no weapon formed against us will prosper and by His stripes, we are healed." Though Shirley could barely walk, so great was the pain, and despite a tumor in her breast that was half the size of a fist, she decided to live by faith and speak not a word of doubt. "I never found one place in scriptures where someone came to Jesus for healing that they were not healed," she told the broadcasters. "I began to see that faith was not just believing that God was able but it was believing that He will." She sought His counsel first and foremost. And that's when, waking from a deep sleep, she saw Jesus at the foot of her bed. "And as I saw Him, I saw compassion, I saw love, I saw hope. I began to feel sweat behind my right knee, and it was so unusual, and I looked at Him and I said, 'Lord, are You telling me to sweat?'"

Remarkably, three days later, visiting a new oncologist, she was amazed when the doctor, Dr. Olivares, a believer, said he had a "word" for her. "I told Shirley she needed to sweat," he testifies—and this she did, beginning sweat therapy that included detox, saunas, and much exercise. She also changed to a strict organic diet. At church, friends fasted and prayed for her, and at home, Mark frequently laid his hands on her and commanded the pain to cease "in the Name of Jesus."

Three weeks after learning about the cancer, Shirley had a dream in which she was standing behind a glass window while a truck careened toward her. She cried out to Jesus and all the huge truck could do was lightly bump against the protective "glass" in front of her. *"That's the cancer I just stopped,"* she felt the Lord tell her.

Two months later, after treatments and her vigorous new routine, she went for a check-up and the cancer was gone. Her doctor told the network it was "a miracle." No tumor. No metastasis. Said Shirley, "I've been healed today because I believed His Word and I took it, and it had to become part of every cell of my being. What He did for me He will do for you."

Approach prayer in a spirit of obedience, abandon, and gratitude, as if the healing has already occurred. Isn't this how Jesus raised Lazarus? (*John* 11:42: *"Father, I thank you for hearing me. I know that you always hear me."*)

It is how—surrender, abandonment—a woman named Chris Carlson came out of darkness and into a healing that was profound. She is an engineer who for a decade and a half suffered from a rare, progressive condition that caused fantastic pain in the face when her skin was merely exposed to bright light or brushed by the wind, let alone touched. It was progressive. Her career had to be set aside. She could barely function. She was in almost constant agony. The slightest pressure would trigger an episode. So hurtful was her affliction—"trigeminal neuralgia"—that many end their lives rather than contend with it; it's also called the "suicide disease"; (an authoritative medical website describes it as "one of the most painful conditions seen in medicine"). Chris and her husband were forced to keep the lights off in her home. They lived literally in darkness!

"It was the most excruciating pain of my life, just pierced straight through my face," Chris recounted (to CBN). Medications and surgeries provided just temporary relief. Finally she pleaded with God—just gave it to Him, in desperation—and was led to a prayer service where a woman named Marlene Klepees, who herself had been cured miraculously of cerebral palsy, before becoming a healer, was ministering.

At first Chris was reluctant—resisted—but finally went up to be "prayed over" by Marlene, who "felt it was important to touch the side of her face" (despite Chris's condition) and say a simple prayer. A tingling—heat—engulfed Chris's face.

"And then, my face just opened up and my eye opened and I had no pain," Chris testified. " It had been fifteen years and it was gone! I was healed only because He loves me." So grateful were Chris and her husband that they left their careers, sold all they owned, and began traveling with their own ministry. It became "the most blessed life." A curse became a blessing.

When, years before, Marlene was healed—of her cerebral palsy—the illness was such that she was a spastic quadriplegic at Mayo Clinic (where they didn't think much else could be done for her). She depended on others to provide for basic needs, with no real control over her neck and head as the illness progressed and she feared being sent—imminently—to a nursing home. This was when she "just yelled to Heaven and I said, 'God, stop! Get me out of here.'"

She then had a vision. It was of the inside of a church. "The church had light-colored woodwork," said Marlene. "The doorknob was a triangular glass-colored doorknob. And then the vision showed me in a rust-colored stretcher and people gathered around praying for me. There was a man in a pin-striped suit.

"Then God showed me a picture of myself out riding a bike on beautiful green grass, and it said 'March 29th' in just great big bold letters. That was three weeks away."

When three weeks passed and nothing happened, Marlene, who also had eye problems, pleaded again with God. In prayer she felt "told" to have her nurse look in the yellow pages under the category of "churches." As the nurse turned the pages for her, one seemed to "glow." On it was a listing for, "Open Bible, Scott Emerson." Immediately she had the aide dial it and spoke with Scott, who hearing what she said decided to come to the hospital. He then took Marlene to the church (after she so strangely described it to him), strapped in her chair (because her body was jerking so violently), and with others asked God to heal the woman from the top of her head to the tips of her toes. Then they asked Marlene—this quadriplegic in a wheelchair!—if, on faith, she wanted to "stand up." *Stand up?* Marlene had never stood. But strength surged into her legs and suddenly her feet hit the floor for the first time in her life and she was standing! Everyone began praising God. His Presence was tangible and with each step her knees and toes straighten all the more. The Lord "told" her to take off her glasses and suddenly Marlene could see clearly. (She never did need glasses again.) Afterwards she was able to hold and eat an ice-cream cone. She shocked nurses by walking in the hospital by herself when she returned. Twenty years later she owns a flower shop and told me it's a busy place; when she can, in her time off, she enjoys riding her bike past lush grass in the country.

7

Spirits of darkness

'The Lord your God turned the curse into a blessing for you because the Lord your God loves you' (Deuteronomy 23:5)

There are countless such miracles. At Lourdes, the first documented healing was of a woman who while pregnant had fallen from a tree, dislocating an arm and ripping through nerves, which caused what was deemed to be permanent paralysis of two fingers. Early in the morning on March 1, 1858, this woman visited the apparition site, met Saint Bernadette, and prayed with the seer. She also bathed her hand in the stream that Bernadette had discovered near the grotto. Immediately the woman could move her fingers again. Another named Pierre Bely was diagnosed in 1972 with multiple sclerosis. His ailment progressed from needing a cane, and then a wheelchair, to total incapacitation. In the fall of 1987, he was able to get to Lourdes, and the day after his visit he experienced a sensation (this time cold) on his skin that morphed into warmth, and slowly but surely Pierre could move his arms and soon after was able to walk again.

Some healings are immediate. Most occur over a period of time. Just as natural remedies may take a while, even a long one, to have their effect, so too do spiritual cures.

Often, what is profound takes time. It is progressive. There may be unseen matters to resolve. It's a mystery—but that healings occur, and astounding ones, is beyond question.

We are *spirit*.

Witness the phenomenon of "phantom limbs": medical literature is filled with accounts of those who've lost an arm or a leg but still feel sensation in it.

It may be an artifact of nerve endings but also may be the spiritual body and it is the spiritual side that is susceptible to sin, curse, and emotions.

Dr. McAll claimed to have witnessed dozens of cases where spirits haunted various locales, causing accidents, disputes, and other negative effects. This gets back to what I said about unclean spirits that may linger over a place and "haunt" a family. "When people move to a new house it is a good idea to have it blessed," said the psychiatrist. "I would go further and include prayers for the whole area in a Eucharist as there may be other lost souls still wandering about and needing help and committal to God."

In a little book called *Exorcism: Encounters with the Paranormal and the Occult,* by Father Jose Francisco C. Syquia, there is recounted the exorcism of a home in Makati, Philippines. Spirits were often seen roaming the ground. At night, an entity seemed to be *in* the house. A religious sister who specialized in spiritual warfare arrived with a team, including Father Syquia. "My first inkling of things to come was when the sister alighted from the van," he said. "She immediately doubled up in pain and started vomiting. I remember looking at her with confusion. It did not yet dawn on me that she was sensitive to the spirit world and was reacting to an evil presence in the vicinity. But I later became more alarmed when she showed the group her arms. Rashes were starting to appear on them! She really looked sick! Although I was still a bit skeptical about a spiritual explanation to what was happening to her, slowly, it dawned on me that these sicknesses may be some form of spiritual retaliation." The deliverance team split up to investigate the vicinity, sprinkling Holy Water. A priest who was with them felt a strange tingling in his arms as he blessed a storage shed (*bodega*). "When we entered the large, dark *bodega*, I could palpably taste the dry and stagnant air in that place," the exorcist in the Philippines, Father Syquia, recalled. "This was a place that was rarely visited except during the times when things had to be stowed away. Even though I was not psychic, I could feel my entire body tingling. The hair on my skin seemed to rise all at once. [The other priest] was silent as he blessed the place. Knowing him to be a talkative person, I knew that he could sense the same eerie feeling I was getting."

When they joined the others, it turned out the second group had located what they felt was the problem. Sister sensed a "malevolent entity that roamed the house at night harassing and sowing fear." It dwelt, she felt, in a "very old mango tree" next door, the branches of which overhung the house. "It's a huge hideous demon," she told them. "It is covered with dark hairy fur." Father Jose didn't know how to react to that claim but the team carried a large wooden olive-wood Cross to the spot and sister hurriedly took it and approached the dark tree. "Suddenly, our jaws dropped," recounted the priest. "The heavy-built sister twirled around like a top in high speed right before our eyes! She desperately tried to gain her balance to keep from falling into the pool which was just a step away. At the last moment, she regained her footing and quickly retreated. She was visibly shaken and had to sit down." Everyone was in shock at what they had witnessed. The sister seemed very weak. She gathered herself. Once more she entered battle with the Crucifix. Better prepared, she issued sharp commands against the spirit, which was given no more opportunity to retaliate or launch a pre-emptive strike. Sister told the priests she saw the shadowy beast flee. "After just a short while, she turned around with a beaming smile on her face and matter-of-factly stated that it was over," recalled the cleric. "I knew for a fact that it was over because all the physical sicknesses that she had when she arrived were gone. She now looked young and vibrant and her demeanor was one that exuded joy."

The entire team felt happiness and peace.

"The majority of physical illnesses are evil working," a healer in Jacksonville, Florida, Father Jose Maniyangat, believes. Once cast out, joy and health come back—be the affliction a rash, nausea, or something more ominous. Darkness leaves like the shadowy beast. But too often it inflicts damage. In the vast majority of cases, spirits aren't recognized and remain hidden (causing "incurable," mysterious ailments). Lack of joy and peace—a feeling of despair—is a marker. (Once more, *oppression.*) So is malaise. "It is important to remember, that if the entities manifesting are of a diabolical nature, then they must be driven out in the Name of Jesus," says Father Syquia. "There is no such thing as a mutual peaceful co-existence with elementals or nature spirits since no one in his right mind would want an invisible liar and murderer filled with hatred in one's home. They will always clandestinely affect the persons in the home in a negative manner, one way or the other, whether through sicknesses like heart attacks, headaches and stomach aches, relational problems and division within the family, emotional and psychological illnesses like impatience, anger, and depression, temptations like lust, pride, and sloth with regard to one's prayer life and Christian obligations; weakening of faith in God, as well as failures in businesses and other endeavors."

There is warfare

Demons are dark.

Spirits that don't go to the light are "unclean."

This, some believe (for our discernment), includes disembodied humans. The victim may suffer dizziness, arthritis, or insomnia plus heart problems and cancer along with a proclivity for accidents, all caused by forces that elude medical perception. A clue: convergence of "unfortunate events." Ailment after ailment is suffered in a particular room, home, or area.

If a soul of the departed is earthbound—avoiding the Light of God—he or she may affect humans in the same way that demons do. Again: Jesus used the term "unclean" when casting spirits of infirmity out of people. If we'd stop and realize how many "psychological" illnesses are caused by spiritual influence, we would clear out half of our psychiatric wards. (I have heard this from nurses who work with such patients.) In fact, the very patient upon whom Sigmund Freud based his first major theory believed that instead of the mental "illness" Freud diagnosed, she was plagued by an entity. (Freud's co-author ended up agreeing with her!) A good guise, this: inventing psychiatric terms for spiritual weakness, which is a reason why there is a poor success rate in psychotherapy (and why many psychologists themselves develop mental disturbances). They call obsession "neurosis"; oppression "schizophrenia"; and possession a "split" personality or "multiple-personality disorder" (the Lord said "legion," *Luke* 8:30).

Mental is mind and mind is spirit. All of the brain is in the mind, but not all of the mind is in the brain. "Anger, resentment, frustration, or a purely materialistic attitude forces the target organ, the blood vessels, to carry the strain," wrote McAll. "Many people use a medical diagnosis as an escape route, excusing their bad behavior by hiding behind labels such as 'my high blood pressure.' Stress results from resistance to the pressures and challenges of life, so where there is no resistance, there is no stress."

Clearing this through Confession, repentance, and expiation, plus forgiveness, often sets one on the path to health. Expiation may mean pain. Use sacramentals. Just as salt and water can be blessed, so can your blood (which is largely just this: water and salt). During the Consecration of His Blood, ask Jesus to bless your blood; ask Him to anoint particular organs. Use blessed oil.

Sacramentals are real. Suffering cancer of the eye, one woman sought the help of Brother André Bessette, the miracle man of Montreal. Thousands were healed by this saint who died in 1937 and his devotion to Saint Joseph. She was told by Saint André to take some oil from the oratory, apply it to her eyes, and offer a daily prayer to Saint Joseph, using a medal of him.

"She went to the altar of Saint Joseph to pray, climbed the stairs to the crypt on her knees, and spent the rest of the day in prayer," wrote Bernard Ruffin. "Within weeks the cancer had disappeared entirely and in August, 1930, a year after the cure, the woman's daughter wrote the oratory to report that her mother was in excellent health."

Reported too was the healing of torments such as addiction.

Once Brother André was staying in the home of an alcoholic. The wife and husband were almost violently arguing (over his drinking). When she tried to stop him from downing a glass of whiskey in front of the holy visitor, the husband viciously cursed and went for his drink. But as Brother André looked on, before it touched the man's lips, the glass shattered! Not to be deterred—and with another curse—the fellow filled a second glass. As Brother André stared, this also shattered! (After a *third* glass broke, the man vowed to give up drinking.)

We see here power that is real. Actual.

A Methodist woman went to see Saint André and the first thing he asked was if she knew Saint Joseph. When the woman, identified in a letter to the oratory as "A. H. Anthony," said she did not, Brother André said, "Well, I can't help you unless you pray to him. Take this holy cord. Tie it around your waist. Take also a bottle of holy oil and rub yourself with this medal, and wear it. And go to the church to receive the blessing."

Despite her Methodist upbringing, which considered sacramentals to be superstitious, Mrs. Anthony did as instructed, entering the church, kneeling before the statue, and weeping with worry and *fervor*. (Fervor is key.) "Saint Joseph, if you want to cure me, I will learn all your prayers and recite them every night, if necessary," the woman promised. "I will honor your statue, without any shame. I will climb the steps [to the oratory] for any favor I ask you. I will never fail to follow you."

Suddenly she was "overwhelmed with the feeling of so much happiness that I began to cry," experiencing a "physical lightness," wrote Ruffin, and "a sense of being freed from illness."

From that moment she was cured of cancer and the torment that comes with it.

8

The Power that closes wounds

'For I will restore you to health
And I will heal you of your wounds' (Jeremiah 30:17).

Take care of the spiritual and according to the Will of God the physical follows.

In our time, with all the malignancies, we must urgently heed this.

"Since we all have cancer cells floating around in our bodies, the key to health is strengthening what happens in our spirit to activate our immune systems," says Dr. Francis MacNutt, an expert on healing who taught at a seminary.

One can tell a plant's connections to good elements—water, soil, and air—by the quality of its yield—"fruits"—and the same is true of us. As the Blessed Mother said (concerning the sick), *"The more you believe firmly, the more you pray and fast for the same intention, the greater is the Grace and the Mercy of God."*

Quality and quantity.

For the power of Christ is love and love enfolds; it penetrates. It closes wounds. It produces. It covers over a multitude of sins (*1 Peter* 4:8). Healing is God's touch and He responds when we purify through compassion. As Mahatma Gandhi said, "God demands nothing less than complete self-surrender as the price for the only freedom that is worth having. When a person loses himself, they immediately find themselves in the service of all that lives." As Jesus said, *"By gaining his life a man will lose it; by losing his life for My sake he will gain it."*

Remember this: cancer feeds on pride; anger grants Satan "territory; the devil builds "strongholds" (*Ephesians* 4:26-7; *Psalm* 106:13-15; 2 Thessalonians 2:11-12); he comes to torment (*Matthew* 18:34-35). We help him when we are bitter. Realize you were delivered by His Blood. Confess. Ask God to reclaim what was surrendered to Satan. Destroy strongholds. Be a conqueror instead of conquered. Identify root cause. When there is temptation, "shatter the glass"; give it to Jesus. Reject sin, but not yourself. Go to Saint Joseph.

In what we have thought, said, smoked, eaten, had to drink, in what we were exposed to as far as chemicals, or viruses, or through genes, or drugs: all of us have weaknesses that can cause issues—health problems—that only God through nature can fix.

Take things as they come. "Ride the waves." My father, who lived to be 93, said this.

Harmony leads to health and health leads to harmony. Work at expelling stress.

The word *"Sha'lom"* from Hebrew means, more than peace, "harmony with the elements."

We might say: harmony with God and His Creation.

I read the account of a woman named Esmeralda Stavra in Symi who was 107 when she died on this island in Greece where they are very physically active, eat the right things, take time for neighbors, get sun, and don't know stress. Her house was at the top of the village steps and even when she was a hundred years old Esmeralda went up and down three or four times a day so she could sell the feta cheese and yogurt she made. She was never ill; never went to the doctor, for so much as a checkup (her children said). She was "harmonious." She was in tune with nature. She was connected to God.

When she died, said her daughter, they "thought she had just gone to sleep—that's how quickly she went."

This is a place famous for the number of residents who, living at peace, and with good, natural food, along with the physical activity, live to be a hundred. They are in the flow of Creation.

When we're in harmony with the natural and spiritual (instead of in opposition to either, or both) health flows through the physical. This doesn't mean conceding to worldliness—the carnal. It means nurturing the body until like a cocoon it releases the soul to Heaven.

Upon that release: *"Sha'lom."*

This is ease.

Sickness is *dis-ease.*

One notes the interplay of nature and Heaven in what causes sickness or well being. See the Bible. There is the way that apples stabilize blood sugar and lower cholesterol (Song of Solomon); that barley (cited in *Ezekiel* 4:9) is high in fiber; that garlic was used as an antiseptic (as well as an antitumor agent) by the time of Moses; that grapes (*Numbers* 13:23) were the first thing Noah planted after the Flood (see the benefits of wine); that legumes (*Genesis* 25:34) stand as another good source of fiber and can help reduce blood pressure; that nuts (including almonds, pistachios, and walnuts; again, the Song of Solomon) bring health; that olives (one of the most valuable trees in biblical times) are so great for their oil; that wheat (see *Jeremiah* 41:8) can strengthen the body (if unprocessed); that onions fight colds and asthma (*Numbers* 11:5); and that fish (mentioned throughout the

New Testament) fights inflammation, heals the arteries, reduces the chances of stroke, and may inhibit cancer. Beans. Lentils. Note the many ways that figs are good for us and how the tree that produces them, umbrella-like, is a symbol for the "protection of God."

Or on the other hand, look at how tobacco, smoked by Indians to conjure demi-gods, causes cancer in the natural; or how hard liquor is called "spirits."

Natural and spiritual interweave.

The "staff of life"—wheat—is used to make the Eucharist.

Cast out evil during the *Lord's Prayer*; during Communion; if the Precious Blood is available, partake. As Saint Augustine said, "It is a victim that we have received and it is into a victim that we are transformed. Every time we receive Christ, we become bone of His bone, flesh of His flesh, humility of His humility, purity of His purity, and holiness of His holiness."

Blood of His Blood.

"The Mass is the greatest prayer of God," Our Blessed Mother once intoned. *"You will never be able to understand its greatness. That is why you must be perfect and humble at Mass. I beseech you, pray to Jesus! I am His mother, and I intercede for you with Him, but everything does not depend solely on me, but also on your strength and the strength of those who pray. The Mass is the most important and the most holy moment in your lives. If you abandon yourselves to me, you will not even feel the passage from this life to the next life. You will begin to live the life of Heaven from this earth."*

9

Back from the 'dead'

'I have healed you and brought up your soul from the grave'
(Psalms 30: 1,2)

And sacramentals?

Many healings involve oil.

Father Nicholas J. Magoulias of St. Paul's Greek Orthodox, in Hempstead, Long Island, was approached by the cousin of an eight-year-old boy named Brian who was suffering from head tumors. According to the church bulletin, which withheld the name of the youngster, Father Magoulias presented the cousin with a vial of oil from lamps that burn near icons of Our Lady of Perpetual Help and the Lamenting Mother of God that shed miraculous tears in the 1960s. The cousin gave the holy oil in turn to the child's mother, who waited two days (after the boy resisted the oil) but then started putting it on him at night while the infirm youngster was asleep.

"A week later the doctors told them that another tumor was growing in the top of his head," the cousin related to parish authorities. "They said they saw it for a while, but thought it was scar tissue until they realized it was growing. So, three weeks after his last operation, he was now [going to undergo] another surgery. The morning of the operation the doctor took one last x-ray. To his amazement the tumor had shrunk considerably, in fact, it was almost completely gone. The doctor told them that he cannot explain it medically and was quite confused that the tumor should shrink so much as to almost completely disappear. He even suggested that he might not even operate. He chose to go ahead anyway. When he opened him up, the tumor was almost entirely gone and what was left were tissues."

Priests at the church told me they receive at least two credible reports of similar miracles each year.

The miracles originally involved icons that shed tears in private homes and were given to St. Paul's. It all began on March 16, 1960. In addition to tears, the eyes on one of the icons were seen moving for hours—garnering world attention (even that of a future president, Richard Nixon)—and when the first icon was processed to church, "a trinity of white sea gulls, soaring against the blue sky over Island Park, heralded the enshrinement of the Madonna of the Tears," reported the *New York Journal-American*—escorting a procession of thirty cars and circling over the church as services were conducted. Hundreds of thousands began to visit this holy church just east of New York City.

Sometimes it is regular oil that has been blessed by a priest. Cures may occur during "anointing of the sick" or during a liturgy. Note that oil is also used during exorcisms—drawing the link, once more, between deliverance and healing. "Several years ago my husband and I were out in the middle of the Atlantic Ocean on a cruise to South America," a friend named Jane Griffin of the St. Louis area wrote me some time ago. "I had picked up a bug onboard and it had turned into a very bad upper respiratory infection. There was no doctor onboard with antibiotics and I was having a lot of pain just breathing. I had to lay in bed just a certain way in order to sleep. I decided to go to the Saturday Vigil Mass on board, and at the end of Mass, the priest announced that if any aboard were old or sick to come for anointing.

"Was I ever happy to go!" said Jane. "He anointed me and I went back to my cabin. At three a.m. I awoke completely well! I recall walking briskly up and down the hall in amazement at this gift!"

Sacramentals?

"I've witnessed a number of miraculous healings through the intercession of Padre Pio," testified another, Don Marrandino, of Brigantine, New Jersey. "About five years ago a man in his late thirties overdosed on drugs and was pronounced brain dead in the Atlantic City Medical Center. When I visited him it was ten days since his parents were told that he was 'brain dead.' I laid hands on his forehead and prayed for Padre Pio's intercession. Within a day or two he came out of the coma and had brain activity. I was told that he made double the progress of anyone that they ever treated. His uncle, who is a surgeon, had told the parents that Tom had a better chance of hitting the lottery than making a recovery! Another time I was visiting my mother in the same hospital and a nun assigned to the hospital asked me to come with her to the trauma center to pray with a seventeen-year-old boy who was in a car accident. We went to the center, where I found the young man whose head was terribly swollen. I placed Padre Pio's oil on his head and prayed for the saint's intercession. Relatives had come from England to be by his deathbed. Although I don't have all the details, he made a miraculous recovery, later attended college, and his mother came to Padre Pio's Shrine in Landisville, New Jersey, to give witness and thanks. I have witnessed a number of healings—pancreatic cancer, a child with holes in the heart, breast cancer."

The horizon brightens when we believe.

"Not only was my husband Louis critical but the hospital treating him tried to euthanize him," claimed a woman who used holy oil. "The doctors never told me about the true nature of his illness—severe atrophy of the mid-brain (the part of the brain that makes you a person). Add diabetes, kidney disease, hypertension, gallbladder disease with gallstones and a tumor, hepatitis, acute pancreatitis, an 'undiagnosed brain injury' (caused by a car accident), severe anemia, with a shower of clots in the brain from a blood clotting disorder. Let's not forget the hypoglycemic episode with anoxic encephalopathy which means very low blood sugar and no oxygen in the brain and multiple strokes causing severe damage. After numerous talks of euthanasia by the doctors, Louis miraculously improved! And today he only suffers amnesia (from the car accident) and diabetes; all other medical conditions have returned to normal! I know that the healing oil changed our lives dramatically."

Tens of thousands have been cured at Lourdes (though only sixty-eight are officially recognized). Even grottos fashioned after the famous apparitions to Saint Bernadette—whose body is partially incorrupt—report healings. I received a letter from John Potocki of Hanover, Pennsylvania, who said:

"I have told this story to one other source as it is difficult to believe, even for me. In December of 1997 I was told that I needed a four-level, cervical corpectomey which is a 'near impossible' surgery that almost always has very nasty side effects. To complicate matters there are not five surgeons in the U.S. who have performed this surgery. I was off work from January 31 to the surgery date in February. During this time I often went to the Lourdes Grotto in Emmitsburg, Maryland. I would get there early on a weekday, generally around eight in the morning. At 7:30 to 8:00 in the morning it is quite cold and there was never anyone there—never. Who goes to a Grotto when it is 15 or 20 degrees out and even colder on the mountain? But one cold morning I was walking up to the Calvary Scene when a young, radiant nun dressed in a habit was walking down carrying flowers. I immediately was struck by her sense of calm and peace; it was overwhelming. Pure serenity! She said to me, 'Excuse me sir, but if you are going to the chapel it will not be open until ten.' I thanked her and told her I was going to the scene of Calvary. I was just deeply moved by her serenity and true happiness. At that time, in my fifty-three years, I had never encountered anyone like this at any time—total peace and serenity. I was thunderstruck. She just exuded an ethereal radiance that was almost beyond understanding. I couldn't tell if she was 22 or 32; she seemed *ageless*. I still can't explain [how she had had flowers in cold weather].

"Well, I went to the Calvary Scene, where I would kneel and pray to either die or make a reasonable recovery. I had the surgery and went through some very difficult months, but the other physicians couldn't believe my amazing condition."

There was also the testimony of a seminarian who had just one eye and had a threatening problem with it. His name was Bob Bailey; he was facing blindness. After visiting the grotto, he was given a clean bill of health.

God often works miraculously but subtly, at special places or your own home, in a way that seems like a natural occurrence. Another friend named Roberta Marziani said that when she discovered a lump on the calf of her left leg, two doctors said if it didn't go away within a month they would have to biopsy it. "I was really upset, and my second visit to the grotto was March 25," said Roberta (who once worked as an editor for *TV Guide*). "That was the day Maryland was founded by a Father White, who landed on St. Clement's Island in 1634, which happened to be the feast of the Annunciation, and named Maryland 'Mary's Land' in honor of Our Lady. Anyway, something told me to go up to a spring where water comes out like at Lourdes. It was cold but I pulled up my pant leg and splashed the water on the lump three times. The very next day the lump started shrinking and by the end of week it was gone.

"The two doctors couldn't believe it."

Roberta added about another visit to the grotto:

"I was just getting ready to get in the car to go home and something in the sky caught my attention. I saw the swirling and I looked and there was this huge, huge angel praying. There was nothing else in the sky but stars and this angel. It was five a.m. This was also on the Blessed Mother's birthday. It was the bottom of the swirling that caught my eye. There were no clouds. The rays in a picture I took look like a white-veil material, and I could see the stars through it. I could make out its head and the wings and his hands, which were in prayer. The head was bowed. This was September 8, 2000. I was just so shocked to see it. I got out of the car three times; I couldn't believe I was viewing this. I could see it for about fifteen miles. That's how big it was. It was coming from the grotto mountain, so huge it just shot up in the sky."

10

When angels come

'He sent His word and healed them, And delivered them from their destructions' (Psalms 107:20)

Angels come when they're called. How often do we call to them? How often do we remember to invoke our guardians for healing?

A few years ago was a case in the news whereby Chelsea Banton, a disabled child in Charlotte, North Carolina, was at death's door from pneumonia. Her family prayed and continued even after the child was taken off life support—never wavering. Meanwhile, the jaws of hospital workers, watching hallway security monitors, dropped when suddenly they noticed strange bands of light (*"a soft white-ness and an infused radiance"*) that looked like a winged being, radiating near the entrance to the girl's room. Just then the girl began to revive.

Angels? Saints?

The accounts would fill a library.

"Lying in a hospital bed after surgery on his spine, unable to walk and in agonizing pain, Jack Sullivan propped himself up on elbows and prayed, not to some vast, unknowable god, but to a specific figure in the Catholic Church, vastly respected, yet mortal: Cardinal John Henry

Newman, an Englishman who died in 1890," reported a
newspaper a few years back. "The healing, as Sullivan tells
it, was almost immediate. He felt a tingling all over, was
flooded with warmth, and, as easy as that, he could walk."

To view the incredible number and variety of healings
which can supernaturally take place, look at the ministry of
men such as Father Solanus Casey (now venerated) of
Michigan.

There was Father Magin Catala, also up for beatification, also American (California).

"Many testified at the hearing that the holy man's
prayers often saved women in desperate cases of child-
birth," stated one expert on his life. "In fact, the unanimous
testimony of his surviving parishioners was that no
woman—during his lifetime or after his death—who had
sought his intercession in a life-threatening delivery ever
failed to obtain a happy outcome. After his death, some
midwives kept relics from Father Catala's habit to use in
desperate cases; they testified before the court that they
never once lost a mother or a child when they invoked the
intercessions of him."

With God, the impossible is matter-of-fact.

Reports a book called The *Bible at the Border* by
Richard Dunstan (detailing the remarkable wonders atten-
dant to a charismatic ministry for the poor in deepest Texas):
"In 1993 Teresa Juarez of El Paso was diagnosed with a brain
tumor. The tumor was an aggressive one, expected to spread
quickly through her body no matter what treatment she
might get. She had headaches and convulsions, she was deaf
in her left ear, and she couldn't drive, or even bathe by
herself. 'The doctor said if I would live three months, that
would be a lot,' she recounted. Still, Teresa agreed to a long,
brutal program of radiation and chemotherapy. About a
third of the way through it, she went to a church across the
river in Mexico and prayed to the Virgin Mary. 'I said "go to

your Son, as in the wedding of Cana (*John* 2:1:11), and ask Him to heal me, or His Will be done,'" she said. Right away, Teresa felt a pulling sensation on her hair. She could hear out of her left ear, and she felt heat throughout her body and head. She blacked out and had to be carried from the church. Later friends said she had cried for two hours. She cancelled the rest of her treatment and went back to her doctor for another brain scan. He agreed only when she signed a release. But the scan found the tumor was gone."

Remarked Teresa: "I haven't had any type of symptom since that moment."

This is the God—our God—of healing.

He operates in our humility, which means littleness.

He makes big out of the small.

He favors those who are marginal.

That littleness comes with unselfishness, for a focus on self blocks Grace.

So many sins—lust, anger, jealousy—go to *self.* (Asmodeus, as in *Tobit*, is thought to be a demon of lust).

It is when we relinquish self and operate in faith that the door opens for the miraculous.

Let's cite another "impossible" case.

Here we have the instance of a young man named Paul Wash, 17, who was driving on an icy highway in suburban Philadelphia in 1983 when he smashed into a tree, causing head injuries so severe that a doctor described them as similar to an egg dropping on cement. Just devastating. *Impossible.* Every single bone in his face was busted and his skull was "shattered," in the words of a writer named Susan Brinkmann. His brain was also ripped. Doctors at Crozier Chester Medical Center laid it on the line: irreversible brain injury. No chance he would regain consciousness.

Fast forward to May of 2005.

That's when Paul received his bachelor's degree from a college in Aston!

One of the physicians, Dr. Michael Ryan, said in a written statement that Paul's recovery was "unexplained on a purely medical and scientific basis," adding that, "it is my feeling that without the help of the supernatural influence, Paul would today be dead or continue to be in a comatose state." His mother Betty had turned to many people for prayer, one of whom had given her five holy cards picturing people up for beatification. Wrote a blogger named Patti McGuire, "Every day after Mass, she and her mother would go to the hospital and pray the Rosary over Paul, then say the five prayers. 'Whenever I came to the Padre Pio prayer, Paul blessed himself, even though he was totally unconscious,' Betty said. Several people witnessed the phenomenon, including a few nurses. Betty called a local group of Padre Pio devotees to report what was happening. They decided to send someone to the hospital with one of the gloves that had been worn by Padre Pio over the bloody stigmata wounds in his hands. On Monday, March 12, Paul was blessed with the relic, and within days, one of his many serious ailments had miraculously vanished. Betty called the group again and on April 6, 1984, the glove was once again brought to Paul and laid on his head. 'I knew immediately something happened because it was like an electric shock went through him,' Betty said. 'He opened his eyes and looked around the room, very clear-eyed. Then he fell back into the coma again but I just knew something had happened.'

"She was right; the next day, when she returned to the hospital she was shocked to find her son sitting in a chair and watching television. He turned and said 'Hi Mom.'"

11

Lean and clean

'I am willing; be cleansed' (Matthew 8:3).

Don't take dis-ease lying down!

In the hospital with tremendous damage from a plane crash, one fellow recalled that "the doctor came back to report the results. Point-blank in his honesty, he told me the tests concluded that my nerves were unresponsive. They were dead and would never return to usefulness. There was a tiny response at one point in my right leg, but it was negligible. The prognosis was that if I walked at all, I would require leg braces and probably crutches. Rejecting that conclusion, I exploded with emotion. I declared [with strong language], 'I am going to walk without using any of that stuff!' I was engaged in a battle, determined to defeat any giant that might stand in my way. I did not know it then, but I found out later that the medical team had already told my family I would never walk again. But I was summoning strength and courage from a Source beyond any human ability. In my weakness the strongest One was releasing power." He walks today with no problem.

Often the miracle manages to be both subtle, gradual, *and* dramatic.

An 88-year-old man named William Lombardi from Clarks Summit, Pennsylvania, who was diagnosed with renal cancer "prayed to Saint Ann and the Blessed Mother and after having all kinds of tests done on my kidney, they decided I didn't have kidney cancer." Now the doctors saw only a cyst, said a newspaper.

Prayers. Novenas. God reacts when *we* act and especially when we have a direct relationship with Jesus. He moves when *we* move. Often we wonder why nothing is happening despite prayer and this can be because we have yet to pray from the deepest recesses of the heart. It has to come from a spiritual reservoir that is fed by His Creative force—which can repair or create or dismantle everything. He is a God Who can create or destroy a universe. All things physical are subject to spirit. All good spirit flows from Him. When we have ill fortune it can be because that flow of spirit has been diverted or blocked by carnality ("flesh") or the enemy.

The power of God comes quickest when we give up "self"; the devil flees humility. Love heals. Pride elevates self, and hates. Pride is a dead-end (though it may have charisma; glitter at first). To be unselfish is to replace lust with love, which heals. When you love, a positive force moves through you while lust is the heat of damage.

Selfishness attracts unclean spirits.

How do we "prepare" a cure? How do we halt an illness *before* it is an illness? How do we protect ourselves and loved ones against the many potential scourges of this life?

Invoke the Holy Spirit and do, eat, and drink what He guides you to do, eat, and drink. Get proper rest. Take plenty of good water. See it as a representation of the *living waters*. Pray over each glass! Start here: water. Drink as much as your body tolerates. Drink green tea. Flush out your system. Grace should be said even over water and snacks. Pray for self-control and it will come to you. Your main sustenance: the Bread of Life. "Because we suffer from a host of food-induced illnesses, we need to develop a healthy diet," wrote a priest named Father William McCarthy. "The well-balanced diet will emphasize fresh fruits and vegetables, nuts and grains, and legumes, plenty of pure water, while avoiding caffeine, carbonated beverages, all processed foods and what dieticians refer to as the 'whites': white flour, sugar and sugar substitutes (honey okay), salt (sea salt and mineral salt okay), milk . . . When selecting foods for your meal menus, remember to avoid combining proteins and carbohydrates in the same meal. If you're having a protein such as fish, for instance, combine it with vegetables. And if you're planning to have a carbohydrate such as whole-grain pasta, again combine it with vegetables. This practice will result in the most effective assimilation of the meal into nutrition and energy while preventing stagnation of the digestive process, leading to the release of poisonous toxins into the system from decaying food. Fruit, when eaten between meals, on an empty stomach, has the added benefit of serving as a cleanser."

Another priest, Father Herbert Burke, found that "organic fruits and vegetables, milk, yogurt, oats, eggs, nuts, nutritional supplements, and regular exercise have helped me maintain fairly good health. If you want to reduce the fat and nutrition-poor calories that make up your body cells, then you need to be on the watch for: fried food, soda, trans-fats, hydrogenated oils, and other junk foods."

Keep clean spiritually and physically.

Eat to live; do not live to eat, especially not what causes "the heat of damage": inflammation. We see that interplay again between physical and non-physical, earthly and other-worldly, hell and Heaven: The word "dementia" reminds us of the word demon—in fact its origin is in the Latin stem word *déméns*—and we see dementia (and even just brain fog) in part caused often by the same pollutants and imbalances that may lead to so many other diseases involving inflammation—imbalances that cause plaque to build in blood vessels (slowing the flow to the brain as well as the heart), that turn the blood to sludge (as too much chocolate and sugar can; "devil's food" cake?), that may contribute even to sciatica or allergies—as we see again the irony of words (and hear accounts of how when used to excess alcohol—spirits—may attract unclean disembodied spirits that seek to re-experience alcoholism). The term "spirits" for hard liquor derives directly from the spiritual word.

What damages the liver also sullies the spirit.

There is the expression "lean and mean," which might be better said as "lean and clean."

For the thinner you are, the more natural the food you eat, the more disciplined, the more physically active, and the more water you imbibe, the cleaner and more efficient is your system including your brain and thus your cognizance. This is health. It is clean—clear—thinking. When the body is "dirty," there's expulsion. This can come in the way of various illnesses and disorders. As strange as it sounds, a cold or the flu and even tumors may be the body's way of purging (or trying to collect and purge) impurities. Refreshing the immune system, which is so important to the function of organs, is paramount. Through bad habits we weaken it and bacteria and viruses just as sin invites darkness. If we are exercising, getting adequate sleep, and eating right, often we can dispel illness without medication.

Very important is fasting, which in addition to cleansing soul and body gives the digestive tract, including the liver, a break. It also allows toxins to be quickly dispelled, working best with good water. There is the "flushing" action. A recent study showed that fasting or greatly limiting food for five days over a certain period can significantly bolster the body against cancer. Spiritually, it's a powerhouse. It potentiates faith. It states a rising above the world (which is under such influence of the devil, the prince of disorder and division, as we see this even in the way that cancer is caused by an alteration—glitches—in cell division). The devil—the flesh—divides, distorts, and conquers, where fasting is unification.

With fasting, healing is set in motion.

When you fast, the body can spend energy and time normally used to digest food on repair instead. Supernaturally, to repeat, the Blessed Mother once said that with it we can *"suspend the laws of nature"*—laws that may be coming against us, in the case of disease and carcinogens. Most effective, said expert Francis MacNutt, is when we lay on hands and pray for each other in the presence of each other—being specific, asking for the Holy Spirit to guide us, bringing in the Blessed Mother, having high expectations, and expressing gratitude. "The most prominent obstacles to our receiving healing are hatred and unforgiveness," MacNutt wrote in a seminal book entitled *The Practice of Healing Prayer.*

Soak in it. Pray for others. The energy behind healing is love (especially of God).

"I was in the deepest state of depression and despair that I have ever known," wrote a woman with basal-cell carcinoma. "Two nights before surgery I was sleeping when I was awakened by a bright light shining in my eyes. I opened my eyes to see a large sphere of light floating about five feet in front of me. There was a light within it that was rotating from left to right. This sphere spoke to me: 'You aren't afraid, are you?' Seeing this light made me fearless. In fact I was filled with the most incredible peace I have ever known. Suddenly the light went through me. It didn't reflect off me or anything like that. It went straight through me. As it did, I was filled with unconditional love which was so complete and powerful that I would need to invent new words to describe it. I asked that my cancer would be removed. I prayed actually. And the light said that what we think of as prayer is more like complaining and we are frequently begging to be punished for something that we are simply going to do again in the future. He asked me to think of my own worst enemy and I did. Then he said to send all of my light to my worst enemy. I did and a sudden burst of light went out of me and returned as if it had been reflected back from a mirror. I became aware of every cell in my body. I could see every cell in my body. It was the sound and sight of light coming from my being. I was crying, laughing, shaking, trying to hold still and trying to catch my breath. When I finally recovered, the being of light said, 'now you have prayed for the first time in your life.'"

12

Claim your blessing

'As many as touch Me are made perfectly whole' (Matthew 14:36)

Nothing is more potent than love and going directly to Christ.

This we get during Mass. It comes at Adoration. It arrives when you offer praise to Him from the core of your being.

He must be standing right beside you. *Thisclose.*

"The Eucharistic celebration is also a time when you can ask Jesus to heal you emotionally of past hurts," points out MacNutt in his book, taking us back to the link between illness and inner wounds. "You simply break down your life into several natural divisions of time, such as year by year, or by childhood, adolescence, young adulthood, and so forth. At home, before Mass, spend some time writing down the blessings that you remember during that year, and then in another column, write down the painful things that wounded you, especially if they were connected with broken relationships, such as with parents or authority figures like teachers. When you are at Mass, make your special intention first of all a thanksgiving for all the good things that happened during that year. Then take the harmful things you listed and ask the Lord, especially as you receive Him in Communion, to bring inner healing to each one."

The laying-on-of-hands helps when done while praying for the Holy Spirit, reciting the Rosary, speaking in tongues, or simply talking to God.

(Take precautions, however, to pray and fast before any laying-on-of-the-hands; discern whether to do it.)

The perfect prayer is simply to have God in mind—Jesus—without ceasing.

You too—by your own prayer—can be healed.

That's not so say there aren't folks who have the special gift of healing but rather to emphasize that with faith and persistence (underscore persistence) remarkable improvements are possible. "For example," wrote MacNutt, "we have seen instances in which the longer we prayed over a cancerous tumor, the more the growth seemed to grow smaller and softer while we prayed until, at last, the tumor was totally gone. How can it be that in the early Church (the first three hundred and fifty years), everyone prayed for the sick, but today most of us can't remember even our mothers or fathers praying with us when we were sick as children? Pope Benedict XVI actively encouraged Catholics to be baptized in the Spirit and to rediscover and experience the charisms, including healing. With over forty years of experience, I've seen thousands of sick people at least get better when we prayed, and some are totally healed. The most extraordinary thing of all is how much healing takes place. Once you actually see what happens to bless your family and friends when you pray, your life (and your family's life) will never be the same."

Jesus said, "Cure the sick, raise the dead, cleanse those suffering from virulent skin diseases, drive out devils" (*Matthew* 10:1, 7-8).

That was to the twelve apostles, but right after it came the same directive to the seventy-two disciples, who basically represent the rest of us.

Heal others. Heal thyself.

"All the marks characteristic of a true apostle have been at work among you: complete perseverance, signs, marvels, demonstrations of power," says 2 *Corinthians* 12:12.

The signs that would be associated with believers, states our Bible, are that we would cast out demons and "lay [our] hands on the sick, who will recover" (Mark 16:17).

As far as tradition, Mary's interventions have involved healing more often than not, including at places such as Guadalupe, where in the midst of her appearances there near Mexico City seer Juan Diego's uncle was stricken with a contagious and deadly fever called *cocolistle.*

Juan gathered herbs and prepared medicine for his uncle, then tended to the suffering man, whose name was Juan Bernardino. This kept Saint Diego from an appointment with the Virgin that day on Tepeyac Hill, where he was to be given the famous *tilma* image.

Still the uncle's condition deteriorated and knowing the fever was so fatal, Juan sprinted to a nearby town called Tlaltelocho to find a priest who could minister Last Rites. Skirting the hill, so as not to be diverted by the appointed apparition, Juan suddenly encountered the Blessed Mother descending at such an angle as to intercept him and in an instant found himself kneeling at her feet. (One can only imagine!)

"Least of my sons, what is the matter?" the Mother of God asked him.

Juan apologized for not showing up as planned and explained that his uncle was dying.

"My little son, do not be distressed and afraid," the *Blessed Mother had replied. "Am I not here who am your mother? Are you not under my shadow and protection? Your uncle will not die at this time. This very moment his health is restored. There is no reason now for the errand you set out on, and you can peacefully attend to mine."*

Juan was soon to learn that Mary was appearing to his desperately ill uncle at the about same time that she was speaking to him.

We see how the supernatural is unlimited by our notions of space and time.

Claim your healing. Claim your blessing beyond natural laws. Case in point: A fellow named Gary Wood was driving with his sister on an icy road when his car crashed. "There was a sharp searing pain that went through my upper facial features," he told a television interviewer named Sid Roth. "I felt a crushing in my larynx. And then I was just relieved of all pain. Dying is just like taking your clothes off and just laying them aside. I stepped out of my body and was lifted through the top of my head over this car and saw my whole life in just an instant. Then I was caught up in a swirling funnel-shaped cloud that grew very bright. Angels took me underneath their wings. They had pronounced me dead at the scene of the accident. I learned that I was dead for over sixty-one minutes. It was ecstasy; it was peaceful; calm, tranquility. Then angels began to sing: 'Worthy is the Lamb Who was slain from the foundation of the world,' and this cloud opened up and I saw this gigantic golden satellite suspended in space what the Bible calls Heaven. It had twelve foundations, and the names of the twelve Apostles were transcribed upon them. There were gates of pearl that were over five hundred miles in width. I started walking on the grassy hill. The grass came all the way through my feet yet there were no indentations. Instead there were diamonds on the grass and an angel standing in front of one of those gates of pearl and he was at least seventy feet tall. He had a sword and beautiful gold-spun hair, and there was an angel inside the city who was holding some books and there was an exchange between these two angels. Then I was allowed access into the city and I have to say I was allowed in the city because I received Jesus Christ as my personal Lord and Savior. I met my best friend from high school who died in a car accident (he had been decapitated) and I certainly recognized him and he began to take me on the tour of the place called Heaven."

During that "tour," claims Wood—near the "throne room" of God—he saw a building with a sign that said "Unclaimed Blessings." In this building as symbols were parts of the human anatomy needed for various earthly healings: arms, legs, organs. "I saw what happened," said Wood. "When people pray the prayers go up and Jesus receives that prayer and He sends out an angel and the angel goes and takes the spare parts and brings it down immediately. Now, sometimes it's instantaneous; sometimes it's like Daniel had to wait twenty-one days to receive his manifestation." When Wood returned to his body (and later, waking up in a recovery room), he found himself with a broken neck, severed vocal chords, missing teeth, a broken jaw, a nose that had been torn off, and the horribly damaged larynx. "Jesus walked into my hospital room—actually walked in; I saw His olive skin, the holes where nails had punctured His hands, the crown of thorns, He had beautiful blue eyes—and He just walked over and put His hands on my throat and smiled and touched me as a song played and then He just walked out of the room," recounted Wood. "He didn't come in by the door; He didn't leave by the door; He is the Door and the little nurse who had been attending me said, 'Good morning, Mr. Wood, how are you this morning?'—just trying to cheer me up. I put up my hands and said, 'Praise God, I've been healed!' (despite having no functioning larynx). She dropped the tray and needless to say she went out to get the doctors!"

When a miracle occurs the veil parts and there is a beam of His Light.

"I have a gift for you," He is saying. "Will you receive it?"

It is from here, beyond the veil—"the place called Heaven"—that the force of healing, sometimes mild, sometimes like a wind, sometimes warmth, or "fire," sometimes gently cool, flows to and through, when healing. "I saw many lights shooting up from the earth like beacons," testified a woman named Betty Eadie, who likewise died and returned.

"Some were very broad and charged into Heaven like broad laser beams. Others resembled the illumination of small penlights, and some were mere sparks. I was surprised as I was told that these beams of power were the prayers of people on earth. I saw angels rushing to answer the prayers. They were organized to give as much help as possible. They delighted to help us and were especially joyful when somebody prayed with enough intensity and faith to be answered immediately. Our thoughts have exceptional power to draw on the negative or positive energies around us. When they draw at length on the negative, the result can be a weakening of the body's defenses. This is especially true when our negative thoughts are centered on ourselves. I understood that we are at our most self-centered state when we are depressed. Nothing can sap our natural strength and health as much as prolonged depression. But when we make the effort to move ourselves away from self and begin to concentrate on the needs of others and how to serve them, we begin to heal. Service is the balm to both the spirit and the body.

"All healing takes place within," she added. "Our spirits heal our body. A doctor's sure hands may perform surgery, and medicine may provide ideal circumstances for health, but it is the spirit that then effects the healing. A body without a spirit cannot be healed; it cannot live for long."

It is when we are in the woe-is-me mode—"I can't endure this," "oh my aches and pains," "look at what I have to put up with," "this is killing me" (all with I or me as the focus)—that we push away healing.

Once a problem comes, once it's identified, the next step must be to verbalize a remedy—to realize that God's Will is always involved but also that we can affect the cells in our bodies when it is okay with Him; or as Eadie put it, "We are not to deny the presence of the illness or problem, we are simply to deny its power over our [spiritual] right to remove it."

When we speak health into our beings there is an excitement among the positive forces around us which then go to work healing, if ordained by God (all in the Name of Jesus).

Heal thyself!

Nothing is impossible for God. I can't tell you how many historical accounts I have studied of miraculous healings associated with statues and appearances of Mary across Europe, especially during the early years of the Church and then during the Middle Ages (at times of plague)— epidemics that often bypassed villages where Mary had appeared or where there was special devotion, perhaps a shrine dedicated to her. There are hundreds of such cases. In South America, an image of the Blessed Mother at Chinquinquirá in Columbia, healed itself of damage—a picture! Can she not help effect a cure for a living person?

And Saint Joseph:

"I saw Brother André kneeling on the floor of the nave of the oratory, at the foot of the Holy Table, enveloped in light, a light coming in a trail from the statue of Saint Joseph on the altar," reported a woman named Adélard Fabre. "It was about 8:30 in the evening. Brother André was completely illuminated. There was only the sanctuary light in the oratory. The statue of Saint Joseph was in darkness but the luminous rays seemed to come from him."

Noted an encyclopedia, "When an epidemic broke out at a nearby college, André volunteered to nurse.

"Not one person died.

"The trickle of sick people to his door became a flood. His superiors were uneasy; diocesan authorities were suspicious; doctors called him a quack. 'I do not cure,' he said again and again. 'St. Joseph cures.'

"In the end he needed four secretaries to handle the 80,000 letters he received each year."

13

Those who live longest

'You will be buried at a good old age' (Genesis 15:15)

Said a doctor who witnessed oil exuding from a miraculous icon in Chicago:

"A great physician or scientist, if honest with himself, is humbled by what little he knows as a function of what there is to know – not just of the human body, but of nature itself, of the universe in which he exists. The infinite order of it all, the intricacy of design of all existing matter, whether alive or inert, boggles the mind of anyone giving expression to such thoughts.

"Through it all, the issue of origin, of ontology, is brought to bear. There had to be a beginning. There had to be a superhuman architect to have fashioned the universe in all of its unfathomable complexity. To me and to the physicians and scientists I've known and respected during my career, that answer can only be God, however expressed by any given person. Under such a premise, it is not hard to reconcile the natural with the supernatural. Things can and do occur for which we have no immediate or rational explanation And just what does, for example, constitute a rational explanation? After all, we learn in science that too often today's wisdom is merely tomorrow's folly."

If healing involves the natural and supernatural—as it does, and as this doctor implies—we must take care of the body as well as the spirit.

Those who do live longest.

It is an area that's ignored by medicine.

Let's look at real examples. Start with Hunzas: Doctors have been investigating them for decades to see what gives these residents of the Himalayas (northern Pakistan) such longevity. They are regularly over a hundred, and some are purportedly a decade or more beyond that. Their diet consists of fresh raw carrots, sprouted legumes, cabbage, whole-grain chapattis, unpasteurized whole milk (yes, they ingest some dairy), a little meat once a week, and lots of pure water. When laboratory rats were fed the same, scientists were startled to find that at the age at which these rodents often die, *none had detectable disease* (and there were no infant mortalities!). The animals seemed happy, alert, and lived harmoniously (in unhealthy circumstances, they fight). When the animals were fed other diets, including one with white rice (as opposed to whole grain, which is how God made it), they developed lung, nose, ear, stomach, reproductive, urinary, skin, blood, heart, nervous system, and lymphatic problems. Hair loss and bad teeth were also noted. An even *less* fortunate group of animals, fed a typical English diet of margarine, sweetened tea, canned meats, white bread, and inexpensive jams, became belligerent and contracted intestinal, stomach, and nervous disease, also prevalent among humans on such a diet.

In the land of the Hunzas, apricots are staples as are cherries, mulberries, and walnuts. Organic vegetables are grown in soil prepared with natural compost. Their proteins come chiefly from beans, legumes, and chickpeas. When meat is taken, it's in small doses from animals ("free-range") that graze in a natural manner. Hunzas also drink that clean glacier water and eat fermented butter and cheese in small quantities. A main drink is apricot oil (which can be purchased in the U.S. and used on salads). The kernel of apricots are full of vitamin B17, which many credit with remarkable cures. As author Tanya Harter Pierce has written, "Researchers over the years have shown similar correlations between diets high in B17 and low incidence of cancer among other native populations of the world as well. These include many of the native North American tribes and native peoples of South America and Africa." Citing another researcher, she points out that "in the Old Testament of the Bible there is specification for how to prepare grains to be used in the making of bread. The formula is presented in *Ezekiel* 4:9 and discusses six ingredients. Five of these ingredients are rich in [B17] content and are barley, beans, lentils, millet, and chickpeas (garbanzano beans)."

We speak much about the miracles of the Lord (and rightly so) yet there are also those natural means He sends to heal, and perhaps vitamins, in natural form, like B17, offer hope for what ails you or loved ones.

There was the case of a 59-year-old woman who, according to a physician named Dr. Philip E. Binzel, came in with a history of a left breast that had been removed due to carcinoma and three positive lymph nodes (a sign the cancer was spreading). This woman was told before seeing Dr. Binzel that she had a "slim" chance of survival, even with strong doses of radiation and chemotherapy.

Dr. Binzel put her on a B17 nutritional program and at the time of his writing she had gone twenty years beyond her prognosis (much longer than the average one-and-a-half years for those in a chemotherapy program).

We take this all under advisement. Remember: certain things work for some, but not others. Nuts may be terrific for most, but cause issues with certain people. When there is a serious condition, a doctor should be consulted. Not everything is a cure for every person and certain things may have cause negative repercussions.

But in some cases it was claimed that more than sixty percent of patients with metastasized cancer survived for more than eighteen years due to B17)!

There is always hope.

There is also prevention.

Watch out for cure-alls—"snake oil"—but be open about alternate or additional aids to healing and pray about it.

Exercise regularly. Live in loving families. Eat a bunch of fruit (in this case, apricots). Moderate alcohol. Drink herbal tea (in long-lived hotspots in the Orient, where the age of one hundred is also prevalent, green tea is cited as a key). Don't overcook. Cut down on frying (unless with oil like that from the coconut, walnut, olive, palm, avocado, or grapeseed (remaining way clear of standard vegetable oil). Flush the system out with natural juices. These and other facts were compiled by Sally Beare in a fascinating book called *Fifty Secrets of the World's Longest Living People*. Says Sally: "The longevity hot spots provide recipes that are not only nutritious but delicious. The rule is to obtain high-quality, fresh ingredients and then to interfere with them as little as possible, so that flavors are allowed to come through. People complain that 'health food' is bland, but health food does not have to mean a piece of apple and a rice cake. The principles are simple: plenty of fresh fruit and vegetables, whole grains rather than refined foods, the right kinds of oil, not too much meat, and short cooking times."

Feel free to use all the onions and turmeric and garlic you like—especially garlic. Few things prevent and heal disease as does garlic, including, many believe, cancer. The array of disorders it can alleviate is fascinating. Researchers at Nottingham University recently claimed to have discovered a thousand-year-old remedy that includes garlic and kills "super-bugs" that modern medicine has a difficult time with. (Notice I say "allegedly"; you must take all these thing into discernment and if seriously ill, to repeat, seek a doctor's counsel.) "The ingredients sound like something from a fantasy novel, but the concoction is now proven to nearly eradicate MRSA (methicillin-resistant *Staphylococcus aureus*)," a newspaper in London reported. "The potion is made from onions, garlic, wine, and oxgall, which is bile from a cow's stomach. Each of these ingredients are useless on their own, but when mixed together they have the power to kill incredibly strong bacteria."

Many other foods could be listed; carrots come prominently to mind; dark green vegetables; squash. Tart cherry juice (it has to be tart, available at super markets) can do wonders in helping you sleep, and sleep is crucial. The point, as Hippocrates said: "Let food be your medicine and medicine your food."

"There has been more written about the wonderful health benefits of garlic than any other food source known," notes author Ty Bollinger to extend our discussion a bit. "Its history dates back 3,500 years. Hippocrates was the first to write that garlic was an excellent medicine for eliminating tumors. Recent studies on garlic have shown that it kills insects, parasites, bad bacteria, and fungi. It also eliminates various tumors, lowers blood sugar levels, lowers harmful fats in the blood, and prevents clogging of the arteries. Researchers have also shown that the organic compound that gives garlic its aroma and flavor acts as a very potent antioxidant. It has been found that [one compound] in garlic reduces the formation of carcinogens in the liver. Dr. Sujatha Sundaram, while a researcher at Pennsylvania State University, found that [this compound] caused bowel cancer tumor cells to shrink and die when transplanted into mice."

Perhaps this is why a community in southern Italy called Campodimele (halfway between Rome and Naples, and heavy on garlic) is called "Village of Eternal Youth."

God's medicine is often found in a natural state.

There are other places as well. There is Okinawa, Japan, which recently boasted the oldest documented person in the world as well as the most elderly without debilitating disease. There the mainstay is whole grains, leafy vegetables, sweet potatoes, and smaller amounts of fish, organic soy products, and pork. (When it is not genetically modified, soy is very beneficial.) Fish a couple times a week is highly beneficial (when it isn't fried, which negates the benefits). These things may not only protect organs and dismiss toxins but bequeath a younger, vibrant look—beautify.

Take time to relax. Exercise. In the land of the Hunzas: hours of dance. They eat no more than required and (referring to how much they eat) call their territory "the happy land of just enough."

"In Christianity we have the Holy Scriptures, what God said from the beginning we should eat," said an eighty-nine year old named Belgrove Josiah from Loma Linda, California, another long-living community. "He gave us the nuts and the grains and the herbs that He placed in the earth. And He said you will do better if you subsist on that type of thing."

Few know that tomatoes are potent against prostate problems, as are unsalted pumpkin seeds. Best spice? Turmeric.

The theme is that people who live long lives are drawing minerals, vitamins, and other nutrients right from the way God fashioned them. They also get sufficient rest (see: the Sabbath) and their work may be long but it is not rushed ("low-intensity") with time for a personal touch and *communicating directly* with others.

Halting stress can add fifteen years to a lifespan; losing weight eight years; and ridding refined sugars, according to a recent study, five years. Vigorous exercise may add *thirty percent* to longevity, it is claimed.

The Hunzas tend to terraced fields all day (exercise, sunshine) while the same is true—physical motion—in places such as Bama County in China where just ten percent of those ninety or older were found to have heart problems and (incredibly) not a single malignant tumor could be found, according to one scientific survey (while another showed an incidence of only four such cases per ten thousand residents).

14

You are designed for health

'Or do you not know that your body is a temple of the Holy Spirit who is in you, Whom you have from God, and that you are not your own?' (I Corinthians 6:19).

You are not destined for cancer.

Even if you've done damage, even if your lifestyle has been negligent—even if you are bed-ridden or obese—you can reverse it with God and His nutrition. He will help you when you start helping yourself.

Let me give you an example of how the Holy Spirit helped me lose weight and change my diet.

It started one day in 1999 when I put myself on a scale for the first time in years and was shocked to see that I registered at more than two hundred pounds. I'd never considered myself "fat." Growing up, I was painfully thin. Throughout my youth, you could count my ribs. My mother used to try to fatten us up with raw egg in milkshakes. When I graduated from college I was about five-feet-ten-inches but weighed just 135.

Years went by, and then more years, soon a couple decades. I noticed a slight paunch but never weighed myself and gave it little thought. Meanwhile, my metabolism had slowed (as occurs with age), and I was eating anything I had the yen for, including ice cream and red meat in whatever volume I fancied.

It was in this fashion, through simple gluttony and neglect, that I was suddenly on the brink of *obesity*.

Stepping off the scale, and upset, I sat myself on the edge of our bed and called for the Holy Spirit to help me lose pounds. Immediately I felt infused with knowledge that came not in words but an "instant knowing" to get rid of salt from my diet; limit portions; and drink as much water as I could.

I did as I was "told" (eliminating virtually all salt, and drinking the water), and in short order I was down to 190, and then 180, and soon 165 pounds, where I stayed for years.

This meant watching every food label for "sodium" content. Besides getting rid of most salt—which causes the body to retain water, bloating you, while drinking a lot of water tells the body it doesn't need to retain as much fluid—I cut down on red meat, greatly reduced dairy products (no more ice cream), and all but eliminated fried food. I also increased the level of daily exercise. I had been swimming most days, and now really went at it. There was also yard work and with that healthy perspiration (which gets rid of excess water and impurities).

Years later, when I put on a few too many pounds—bolting up to 175— I went back at it, this time ridding most white sugar and totally banishing high-fructose syrup, as well as more closely watching salt. Salt, fat, and sugar. Even cereal can be loaded with sodium. It was astonishing how at times I put on three or more pounds overnight by simply eating something that had salt or dairy in it. Meanwhile, I had been drinking canned iced tea that I thought was healthy without noting that the level of high-fructose in a tall can was comparable to *seventeen* teaspoons of sugar.

By now focusing on sugar and white flour, I dropped to the "ideal weight" for my height of 153.

Although the pounds fluctuate, especially when I go to a restaurant, I am about fifty pounds less than I was when first I went to the Holy Spirit.

Where I used to have a supply of antacids on hand (always next to the bed), they were no longer necessary.

15

Transcending the physical

'And this woman, a daughter of Abraham as she is, whom Satan has bound for eighteen long years, should she not have been released from this bond on the Sabbath day?' (Luke 13:16)

With God, we transcend the physical, which left on its own always tends toward falling apart ("entropy").

We all die to the physical but should seek to live as long as God has designed for us.

Darkness can prevent this.

"One day a new patient was delivered to our ward," a nurse in New Zealand recounted. "The main nurse told me that he had terminal cancer and that he had only two more weeks to live. He was lying in his bed completely pale; half of his face was covered with a bandage as the cancer had eaten up his upper jaw. The man had to be fed with a syringe and was on morphine. I avoided his contact for some days, as the sight of him caused me discomfort and shudders."

Soon, however, this nurse—an active Christian—felt "called" to pray for the man and did so by "binding" and casting out the "spirit of cancer"—declaring against the seed, root, and cells of that disease; laying hands on the patient; and commanding every malignant cell in his body to die (along with ordering his bone marrow to produce healthy blood and verbally directing tissue affected by the cancer to regenerate). In two weeks the man was back to walking on his own and was dismissed from the hospital soon after.

In many such cases, there is a point of access through which darkness enters.

The occult. As I said, hatefulness. Greed. Lust. Jealousy.

Darkness comes through transgression because when we transgress we're putting a God at a distance.

The farther away He is, the farther away is the healing power of Grace.

Wellness is the opposite of hate.

What are the health effects (fruits) of promiscuity, homosexuality, drug use, prostitution, alcoholism, and gluttony? We all know about cervical cancer and AIDS.

The word "malignancy" comes from "malign" which means "evil in nature."

Are there innocent victims?

There are. Suffering is often sent for mysterious reasons. I don't pretend to know all causes. We have no idea—no matter what we do or don't do—how long we will live. But we can recognize certain rules and ask: do greed and gluttony promote good health; does pride; money?

"I was truly beginning to understand the power of the spirit over the body, and I saw that the spirit functions at a level most of us are not aware of," said Betty Eadie. "The spirit communicates with God, being the receptive device that receives knowledge and insight from Him. It was important for me to understand this, and I envisioned that this would appear much like a fluorescent light tube in our bodies. When the light is glowing, our core is filled with light and love; it is this energy that gives the body life and power. I saw also that the light could be diminished and the spirit weakened through negative experience—through lack of love, through violence, sexual abuse, and other damaging experiences. By weakening the spirit, these experiences also weaken the body."

What is sinful, lacking, or overdone—off kilter—leads to disease.

This takes us back to ego. A focus on "self" disorients and blinds us. It is the self that causes us to want and want and *want* some more, whether money or alcohol or a food like sugar.

This is a lack of discipline and discipline is a key to both spiritual and physical well-being. As such, it is a key to happiness.

Discipline reins in emotions that are unhealthy.

There is a reason why the cardinal transgressions are known as the seven "deadly" ones.

Where does sloth come in?

Sloth is behind a lack of exercise. It is the lazy way of fast food.

Where does anger enter it?

It can burn a hole in your stomach.

Did you know that in the thesaurus other words connected to "cancer" and "malignancy" (in a tertiary definition) include: "spell," "scourge," "bane," "curse," and "voodoo"?

Our most acute problems come from those "curses" that we impose on ourselves.

Spirits can affect our subconscious and it is in the subconscious that we frequently detect them. Sometimes, the baggage of an entire family seems to fall on a single person. This can be because they have done something to deserve it (opening an "access point") or because they were chosen to redeem others (through suffering).

"Dementia and Alzheimer's are perhaps the two most dreaded diseases associated with aging in our society," claims one deliverance minister (for discernment). "It has been estimated that half the people in this country who reach the age of eighty or older will be afflicted with one or both of these diseases. In most cases, dementia and/or Alzheimer's are the result of a disease such as Huntington's or Parkinson's, faulty or inappropriate medication, recreational drug use, heavy metals in the brain, or heredity. But I have recently discovered that in some cases demonic harassment can be a factor. I have had occasion to address this for two women thus far. One was suffering from both Alzheimer's and dementia. The other was in the early stages of dementia. The first was in her late eighties. The second had just celebrated her ninetieth birthday. Both were Christians, and neither had ever dabbled in the occult. In both cases, there were ancestral spirits of dementia, Alzheimer's, short-term memory loss, and confusion. In both cases there were also demonic spirits who had claimed possession of the portions of the brain associated with (1) Intelligence, Judgment and Behavior (2) Memory, and (3) Language. In addition, in each case there were ancestral spirits linked to dementia and Alzheimer's who were depleting and/or interfering with assimilation of Vitamin E, Vitamin B12, Vitamin B6, folate, and iron. For the woman with Alzheimer's, casting away the spirits in Jesus' name that had caused it appeared to have little effect. Apparently too much brain damage had already been done. For the woman with early dementia, 'cast aways' resulted in a significant improvement. If you, a parent, or a grandparent are experiencing the initial stages of dementia and/or Alzheimer's, it would be worth your while to address whether there are spirits of Alzheimer's, dementia, memory loss, and confusion that have been passed on to you."

Far out? Many problems in family lineages, claimed Dr. McAll, can be traced to hidden sin. This is what "occult" means: hidden. "A mother seeking help for her anorexic daughter admitted the fact of an abortion, apologized to God, and in prayer committed the baby by name," Dr. McAll once wrote. "Not only was the girl's anorexia healed, but the mother's constant headaches suddenly ceased. Several examples have a combined therapy, where there are family patterns of migraine. One such, a forty-year-old woman, was the fourth generation of sufferers. The proof of origin came after Confession and absolution because family members in each of the previous three generations had dabbled in the occult. Early in our inquiries we found that a number of anorexic patients had histories of one or more abortions, miscarriages, or other unmourned deaths in their immediate families. They recovered rapidly when the family ritually mourned these deaths. If there were signs of unresolved grief, the patient and the family were helped to look objectively at the relevance of such grief to the symptoms. Thus, they understood that these symptoms correlated with the situation of the unmourned person – that is, lost, lonely, darkness, depressed, unloved, nameless, unable to eat or cry out. A man of forty-eight (who had been diagnosed as schizophrenic) was delighted that after thirty years of treatment, someone asked him for details of his hallucinations. He explained, 'Lots of men are killing each other with swords; there is blood everywhere, a roaring sea, wind on my face, the smell of sulfur and blinding flashes.' It was discovered that he was the direct descendant of pirates and naval captains. The man was released that same evening after prayers and two days later the family attended a Requiem Mass."

"The evil one has the power to cause physical and mental illness," wrote Father Gabriele Amorth, the famous exorcist. "The two most commonly affected areas are the head and the stomach. Usually, the sickness is persistent. At times, though, it is transitory, lasting only the length of the exorcism. Many times women have come to me before undergoing surgery for ovarian cysts, which were diagnosed following a sonogram and the description of the pain. After the benediction, the pain stopped; a new sonogram showed the absence of any cyst, and surgery was canceled. [Another exorcist] can document numerous cases of grave illnesses that disappeared simply with his 'blessing,' including medically verified brain tumors. I must caution that these incidents can happen only to people who are subject to 'negativities,' and by this I mean cases whose origin is of suspected evil origin."

The evangelist Derek Prince wrote about a woman whose hands were healed as a byproduct of praying for release of a curse.

Repeated or chronic illnesses, taught McAll, or barrenness (as well as being accident-prone), can have spiritual roots. Spirits attach to people and also to things. When folks go on "ghost" tours, they may suffer headaches, dizziness, nausea, and faintness; this was noted in one "haunted" place in Savannah, Georgia. Can something worse be transferred? We must always be aware of our spiritual as well as natural environment. One woman from Newburyport, Massachusetts, related how, in her historic, problem-plagued home, "antiques purchased for the children as they grew would cause nightmares. We bought a 1700's rope bed for our son. He started spiking mysterious 104-degree fevers. We were constantly rushing him to the hospital. He started telling us about the people who would come and play with him when he was sleeping. After about a year of this, we got rid of the bed, and the fevers and 'visits' stopped."

16

The road map of your life

'Then your light will break out like the dawn, And your recovery will speedily spring forth' (Isaiah 58:8)

It may seem like a tailspin, but God is in control, always.

When you are desperate, He is there yet closer.

When there is darkness, His Light is brighter.

He has the road map of your life.

When you don't know chemistry, He does.

The famous brain surgeon, Dr. Ben Carson, a presidential contender, recounted the time at Yale when he was failing chemistry and begged the Lord for help, then fell asleep. He had planned to pull an "all-nighter." He was desperate. As he told a national prayer breakfast, "You can't be a pre-med and fail in chemistry." He prayed, saying, "Lord, medicine is the only thing I ever wanted to do . . . Would you please tell me what is it you really want me to do?" In his sleep came a dream and in the dream he was alone in an auditorium and a "nebulous figure" was writing chemistry problems on a blackboard. "When I went to take the test the next morning, it was like *The Twilight Zone*," Dr. Carson recounted. "I opened that book and I recognized the first problem as one of the ones I dreamed about! And the next, and the next, and the next, and I aced the exam and got a good mark in chemistry."

Spirits good and bad surround us. Notes a deliverance expert, "Demons, when they are present, do not just affect the body but also the spiritual life of the individual. Do the infirm have peace even though they are sick? If they feel at ease, even when afflicted, then most likely the disease is natural. There is probably no demon involved. I often look to find evidence of spiritual growth. If it is occurring in the sick person, then their disease seems to be of natural causes. On the other hand, if the sick are being hurt spiritually, then the disease could have some demonic roots."

At Lourdes were seen both the spiritual combat and remarkable healings.

At the start of those apparitions, Bernadette reported howls and other commotion as the devil tried to control the little cave. There was a storm. There was a clamor, meant to frighten. The Lady in White predominated, however, and began a place of fantastic documented healing.

The devil was cast out.

The last officially recognized cure there (the sixty-ninth, surpassing all those nearly impossible scientific hurdles) was to Danila Castelli, born in 1946, wife and mother, who had lived a more or less normal life until the age of 34 when she started having spontaneous and severe blood pressure hypertensive crisis.

"In 1982 some Rx and ultrasound tests detected a right para-uterine mass and a fibromatous uterus," states the official Lourdes medical site. "Danila was operated for hysterectomy and annexectomy. In November 1982 she underwent partial pancreatectomy. A scintigraphy the following year proves the existence of pheochromocytoma (a tumor that secretes high amounts of catecholamines) in the rectal, bladder, and vaginal region. More surgical interventions followed in the attempt to stop the triggers to the crisis until 1988 but with no bettering at all. In May 1989, during a pilgrimage to Lourdes, Danila got out of the Baths where she had been immersed and felt an extraordinary feeling of well-being. Shortly after she reported an instantaneous cure to the *Bureau des Constatations Médicales de Lourdes* (Lourdes Office of Medical Observations). After five meetings (from 1989 to 2010) the Bureau certified the cure with an unanimous vote: 'Mrs. Castelli was cured, in a complete and lasting way, from the date of her pilgrimage to Lourdes—twenty-one years ago—of the syndrome she had suffered and with no relation with the treatments and the surgeries she received.'"

She has since gone back to a normal life.

Science cannot explain it.

Notes a recent testimony (from elsewhere), "People in our assembly laid hands on me and prayed for me and my right leg grew out; however, it was still about half-an-inch shorter than my other leg. Some time later, I decided to pray and lay hands on my shorter leg by myself . . . In 'Jesus Name,' I commanded my right leg to grow and the hips, knees and ankles to be leveled out with the left leg. After the prayer I could feel movement in my right leg, which felt like someone stretching it! I checked the length of both legs and immediately realized that the right leg was exactly like the left leg. There were no more differences in the length of my legs, and my hips and joints and everything were completely level. When I got up, I found myself standing evenly and could feel that my bodyweight was evenly distributed on both legs. The pain in my knees, hips, and back completely disappeared after the healing!"

Is a miracle in store for you or someone you love?

The supernatural rules over the natural.

It may take time—just as it so often takes an affliction time to develop; just as a problem may grow gradually—but God operates in accordance with a Plan.

"The Lord will not grant you the grace of physical sight unless you first receive sight for your soul," Saint Pio once said to a blind man. "After you are baptized, then the Lord will give you your sight." (Gradually—after converting to Christianity—his sight returned.)

Start your prayer by praising God. Prayer will bring you to a healthier diet. The more you pray, the more you'll know how to pray for what you need; the more you'll receive clarity. Get strong—tough—in your supplications. Shout it out, if necessary. Recalled a woman whose son nearly died in an accident, "I would stand by his bed and sing and tears would just roll down my cheeks. The only thing that I would allow to be prayed over him was the Word of God, which is the ultimate authority." She would say, *"I declare, Father, in the Name of Jesus, that You said by Your stripes, Jeremy is healed. Jeremy, I say you are healed and you will fully recover!"* (The boy made a remarkable recovery.)

Open your heart. Look up, not down.

Take the initiative.

A nurse who had cervical cancer changed her diet, ate smaller portions, and reduced her intake of fatty, refined foods, and processed foods. Her diet became a simple one of whole grains and beans. With it she freed herself from the threat of cancer. In the process, her chronic lower-back pain, stuffed nose, blocked sinuses, psoriasis, and pre-menstrual syndrome also vanished (and she was able to lose weight; being overweight is a major factor in cancer).

Always, pray for the right doctor.

Light overcomes darkness—when we let it.

A fellow on chemotherapy insists he "woke up in the middle of the night one night, and just as clearly as I'm speaking to you right now, I heard God tell me, *'It's over. It's finished. It's done. Stop taking the treatments.'* The peace of God was on me, and I said, 'God, You told me to do it, so that's exactly what I'm going to do.'" He was healed.

Said a woman named Gill from St. Albans in England, "As soon as the suspicion arose that I might have cancer I started to look into natural remedies and changed my whole diet accordingly. I believe that this change in diet, fresh-vegetable juicing, and taking nutritional supplements which are known to fight cancer really strengthen my immune system and helped me cope with all the stress of being in and out of hospital for examinations and scans. It took only days from diagnosis to referral and meeting my consultant who looked after me and drew-up my treatment plan. Praise the Lord, God answered my prayer and my consultant was a 'God send.' He confirmed again that I had cancer of the cervix and that the normal treatment plan would be surgery followed by chemotherapy and radiotherapy. I told him that I am a spirit-filled Christian and that I believe that God will heal me completely and that I do not want to have chemotherapy or radiotherapy. At the same time I told him about all the natural remedies I was taking and that I wanted to continue with this approach. At no point did he go against my wishes and was very supportive, even stating 'I want you to be happy and comfortable with the treatment you receive . . . This really gave me peace of mind and confirmed to me that God was with me all the way. After a great deal of prayer, I decided to have surgery (a hysterectomy), but no other medical treatment whatsoever. My consultant referred me to different specialists for scans and MRI. I was scheduled for surgery in mid-April and he wanted to make sure that the cancer had not spread. When I went in for surgery the Lord provided me with nurses and other medical staff who looked after me and comforted and encouraged me to keep my eyes on God, particularly when none of my family or friends could be with me. The surgery went very well and the following day my consultant remarked on how well I looked and asked if I had a blood transfusion as I did not look pale. Later my consultant, who had been my surgeon, stated that he was very surprised that the tumor had not spread and was in fact smaller than what was shown in the scan. As I opted against any further treatment he removed the surrounding glands to be sure that the cancer was completely removed. To the surprise of the nurses and doctors I recovered very quickly and without any complications. A couple of weeks after surgery we were called in to see the consultant to receive the results of the biopsy of the removed glands. The consultant was astonished to discover that all the glands were completely free of cancer, and he believed then that a shadow in the lung had nothing whatsoever to do with cancer. I believe that the Lord worked this miracle and shrank the tumor to a much smaller size and destroyed the cancer lurking in my pelvis. At the moment I have to go in every six months for a check-up, but I have received a letter from the hospital stating that there is no concern that the cancer will return!"

17

Humility draws the help of Heaven

'Therefore, confess your sins to one another, and pray for one another so that you may be healed. The effective prayer of a righteous man can accomplish much' (James 5:16)

Breathe in the Holy Spirit. Get strong. Surround yourself with the saints. Seek nutrition. Go to Saint Raphael. Ask for special healing angels.

If God does not heal, take the pain, embrace it with love, and work your way into a higher eternal place with it. When we suffer well all *is* well—although first we should seek His aid and cast darkness out, in case darkness is at the root.

When you are at the end of your rope, let God take the "rope" and throw you a life preserver with it.

Dizziness. Vertigo. Banish these. Headaches. Pains in the joints. Diabetes.

Even at death's door, a Hand will come down to you.

With fasting and prayer , you can get out of situations that have "no exit."

In the wreckage of one car in a horrible accident (but from which a young man miraculously survived, but should not have been able to escape) the letters "G-O-D" were formed by the twisted metal. His father sent a picture of it.

Maybe it's just swollen feet.

Claim a healing.

Says *Jeremiah* 29:11-13, "For I know the plans that I have for you, plans for welfare and not for calamity to give you a future and a hope [declares the Lord]. Then you will call upon Me and come and pray to Me, and I will listen to you. You will seek Me and find Me when you search for Me with all your heart. I will be found by you and I will restore your fortunes."

It's when we stray from our missions in life that "speed bumps" or roadblocks are often sent and sometimes these may come in the form of ailments.

God is always there. In Ireland, a boy from Galway whose cancer had spread from his bones to his lungs and lymph nodes was free of cancer after a healing that began at Medjugorje. He had been under hospice care. He said he saw a statue of the Blessed Mother move. All the while his father had the impression of a large powerful Hand over the boy's head.

The imagination perceives what the eyes cannot.

It's when we let go and tell God it's okay—whatever He wants, we are happy to go with Him—that He often acts.

He acts in our surrender.

He also acts when we *offer ourselves.*

He acts in obedience (which is more powerful than sacrifice, *1 Samuel* 15:22).

Offer yourself to Him, completely.

This is most powerful.

Abandonment brings angels.

I read about a fellow who had a tumor in his chest the size of a grapefruit.

After prayer, it disappeared.

Very often it's a combination of changes in lifestyle, medical intervention (chemotherapy may be crucial in some cases), and prayer. Days to live? Make that years. *Years?*

Reject the evil report.

Make that decades.

When the disease leaves, often so do faults of the spirit that led to the physical weakness. There is a "correction." We're purified. When they go, the "inherited" illness also is dismissed.

One woman whose grandmother died of a brain hemorrhage at age forty-one herself suffered a serious hemorrhage and said, "I had just completed teaching my weekly CCD class at our Catholic Church. Everything was wonderful! After class, I met with one of the other teachers and we had a brief discussion. It was joyful and pleasant. All of sudden I could not hear a word she was saying. Also, my hands and feet felt numb. I turned and ran to my car so I would be home with my beloved family before things got worse. Driving down the street towards my home, I thought the top of my head was going to explode! I could not continue driving so I had to pull into a driveway where a friend lived with her husband, who is a doctor. At that point, I collapsed and landed on the horn. My friend ran out with her husband and that is all I remember until many days later."

Everyone she knew started praying and she recovered despite a "death sentence" pronounced by her doctor.

Hidden causes there are. No doctor can see them. Said a woman who was praying with her son (to deliver him from asthma), "The Lord then showed me that I needed to let go of this burden I was carrying for my son. He told me this was not my fight. This was my son's battle against evil, and the Lord and his angels would fight it. I realized that my worrisome attitude had nearly turned into a state of depression and was not helping anything. Visually, I let go of the burden. I envisioned myself laying my son's illness at the foot of the Cross." Soon the boy was "101 percent" free of severe allergies (and "asthma").

"Every day I see people who are experiencing some type of possession, some manifestation of the spiritual battle," a Catholic psychiatric nurse-practitioner from Georgia, Kimberly H. Littrell, president of the Promedical Psychiatry Group and Research Center in Loganville, told me. "There are things that are clearly out of the diagnostic categories. Most people in the field want to give it a nice psychiatric code and move on. But the enemy is not just imbalances in dopamine and serotonin [neurotransmitters]. It is Satan." In one case, says Kimberly, a strange voice challenging the nurse erupted out of a woman who had an abortion. In another, a patient coughed up a nail.

When there is attack, or pain, in our lives, often God is calling us to reflect and re-evaluate. He wants to draw us closer. Once we get back to who we really are, there is well-being (even, as I said, with suffering). Perhaps He is indicating to us a weakness through which yet greater problems may enter.

When the priest elevates the Precious Blood, plead for Him to break bondage.

According to Father Hampsch, "troubles in love, financial problems, marital difficulties, anxieties, tension, depression, obsession, and other sufferings may in some cases be rooted in the forgotten or never-recognized past. Many persons are afflicted with excessive fears and phobias or aversions, rage, anger, resentment, outbursts of temper, pouting, overwhelming sense of guilt feelings, addictions to drugs or alcohol, many types of sexual perversions or sexual drives that are very difficult to control, strong temptations to infidelity and fornication, adultery, many types of relationship problems that affect deep levels of the psyche. Sin is both contagious and hereditary. Yet, it is not really correct to say that sin is contagious or hereditary. It is really only sin's consequences that are contagious or hereditary." Most damaging, says Hampsch, is the occult, which "will invariably have serious consequences within the family tree."

It's not always spirits. "I learned," claimed Eadie, "that all thoughts and experiences in our lives are recorded in our subconscious minds. They are also recorded in our cells, so that not only is each cell imprinted with a genetic coding, it is also imprinted with every experience we have ever had. Further, I understood that these memories are passed down through the genetic coding to our children. These memories then account for many of the passed-on traits in families, such as addictive tendencies, fears, strengths, and so on."

If so, these too must be cleansed through the Blood of our Lord.

Bring Jesus into your midst.

Beseech Him for a personal relationship.

As Father John Hampsch, an expert on generational healing from California, and trained as a psychologist, points out, the fact that some ills have a spiritual root hardly means that they all do; I must underscore this. He notes that when Jesus' disciples asked, "Who has sinned, this man or his parents that he was born blind?" the Lord answered (*John* 9:3): *"Neither this man nor his parents have sinned, but this happened so that the work of God might be displayed in his life."* We see here that Father Hampsch is not advising you to forsake regular medical care but rather offering an additional possibility for healing "intractable" illness.

"Sometimes specific ailments are assigned to specific sins, for example, the offspring of adulterers are often infertile, or die young (*Wisdom* 3:16), and the descendants of those who practice bribery often have defective eyesight (*Job* 17:5)," claimed the priest, who has spoken and celebrated healing Mass in all fifty states and more than thirty nations. Many are the biblical references, he notes, to the handing down of the wages of sin. "The fruit of your womb will be cursed," says *Deuteronomy* 28:18 (referring to those who do not obey the Lord). We need not live under oppressions from the past, concludes Hampsch. "When persons give their lives over to God and repudiate the sin in their lives, they can dispose God to break the curse, and in the place of that, the blessing of the Lord is manifested." He suggested that those who think they may be afflicted pray to recognize any such problem; repent of and confess all sin and failures; confess the sins of ancestors (*Leviticus* 26:40, *Nehemiah* 9:2 and *Psalms* 106:6); grant forgiveness to all members of the family tree; pray a prayer of deliverance over past generations; appeal to God for healing angels; and place the Cross of Jesus between each of the generations (asking Jesus to pour His precious Blood through each stratum and destroy negative patterns). The priest further says that the most powerful time to do this is at Mass during the Consecration, during the lifting up of the species, when the great "Amen" is sung, during the closing Eucharistic prayer, and just after receiving Communion. A family chart with the names of ancestors to the third or fourth generation can be placed on the altar. This should be followed by frequent Bible reading, great persistence in resisting evil inclinations, and—when temptation does come—recitation of the Lord's Prayer, which is a prayer of deliverance.

The Lord heals through His Sacred Heart.

He stands there next to you, when you ask Him to.

Paint the picture of health on the canvas of your anatomy and attack what blocks you. Stress. Anger. Resentment. Pride. Pride feeds cancer in the same way that sugar does. Pry these out. Dispel them. They are decay that attracts rodents.

As Saint Teresa of Ávila wrote in *Interior Castle,* "I do not know if I have explained this clearly: self-knowledge is so important that, even if you were raised right up to the heavens, I should like you never to relax your cultivation of it; so long as we are on this earth, nothing matters more than humility. And so I repeat that it is a very good thing—excellent, indeed—to begin by entering the 'room' where humility is acquired rather than by flying off to the other rooms. For that is the way to make progress, and, if we have a safe, level road to walk along, why should we desire wings to fly? As I see it, we shall never succeed in knowing ourselves unless we seek to know God: let us think of His greatness and then come back to our own baseness; by looking at His purity we shall see our foulness; by meditating upon His humility, we shall see how far we are from being humble."

Humility draws the help of Heaven.

Yes, saints intervene. As first reported in *Newsday*, then in a publication called the *National Herald*, "In 2013, Michael approached Father Dimitrios Moraitis, formerly of St. Paraskevi Greek Orthodox Shrine Church in Greenlawn, New York, wanting to walk his guide dog around the church property. Unbeknownst to Michael, in the Greek Orthodox Church, St. Paraskevi is the patron saint for health, specifically of the eyes. In the late 1960s, a family from the Church built a shrine in the saint's honor and brought back holy water from a natural spring that flows from a church built at the place of St. Paraskevi's martyrdom in Asia Minor. Both St. Paraskevi and the water were thought to have healing powers. Since the shrine's conception, hundreds of people have reported receiving miraculous cures from the holy water, Moraitis told Ancient Faith Radio. Moraitis invited Michael to walk the property and invited him inside the church for a prayer service and anointing. When Moraitis put his hand on his head and read a prayer, he says a vibration went through his body and Michael shuddered. They both cried, as Moraitis helped him up and led him to the shrine for another service. After Michael washed his face with the Holy Water, Moraitis says he took a step back and said, 'There's a woman here!,' pointing at the icon of St. Paraskevi. He turned to Moraitis and remarked, 'I see the color of your eyes! I haven't seen a color in seven years and I see the cross over here and I see this round icon.'"

Michael's doctor was dumbfounded.

There is the case of a woman from Long Island who had a short leg. This occurred at Medjugorje. She went on to explain that on Tuesday evening during the apparition (which at that time was taking place on the left tower of the church), "she happened to be standing at the door to the tower; and her left leg, from her knee through her thigh, began to burn," said a woman named Aidan Kane, who saw her. "And the burning sensation continued right up until the Consecration at the Mass, which could have been an hour. And after the burning sensation ceased, her legs were the same length! She told me this story, but she said that it wasn't the whole story. She said that was only the physical miracle! The actual miracle in her situation was a healing of the memory, the healing of a guilt that she carried for some thirty years. Back then, she was going to a disco in Dublin with her sister (she was about fifteen or sixteen) and a drunk driver ran into them. The sister was killed outright, and as a result of the accident, the growth in her leg was stunted. She carried this for thirty years, this guilt [of surviving what her sister had not]. So not only did she get the healing of the memory and of the guilt, but she also got the growth back to her leg!"

In prayer go deep inside and determine: what you are anxious about (and why), who you are mad at, what you fear, why you fear it, who you need to forgive. (It's fear that causes most anger.)

Ridding guilt, anger, or anxiety can also prevent illness. Stress is a huge culprit.

Are there too many deadlines in your life? Are there "dead bones" (*Matthew* 23:27) in your thoughts? Put worries in a box and hand the box to Jesus.

The God of miracles is the God of cures. Sometimes He will raise up a mere layman—and not necessarily even a very believing one—to ministry (as Saint Paul was). Focus on Light, not darkness.

I knew a fellow from San Diego named Bob Rice who was raised Baptist but was not very practicing. A truck driver, one day, out of the blue, he heard a voice telling him to look for a certain mission in the bad part of town and go there. It was such an unusual circumstance that he listened. This was a voice he *heard*. It woke him up. It's what they call an "auricular locution."

Bob, a former Marine, set out for the locale he heard, the Full Gospel Rescue Mission. When he got there he realized he was at a place he didn't even know existed! He introduced himself to the pastor, who then shocked Bob by announcing to his small congregation that Bob was going to get up and speak! Rice took to the pulpit without a notion of what to talk about or even how to formally pray. He simply obeyed an interior force that now propelled him. "I had absolutely no clue what I was going to do," he said. "When I got to the pulpit I opened my Bible and just laid it down on the pulpit—opened to no particular place, because I didn't know anything about it. I prayed a very simple prayer, telling the Lord these were His people and that if there was anyway He could use me, there I was. Use me. I then had this thought going through my mind. I didn't know if it was Scripture or something I had read, but there was this thought going through my mind, and when I looked back down at my Bible, I couldn't believe my eyes: I began to read the same words going through my mind. It was *Mark* 16:17, where it says signs shall follow those who believe, that 'in My Name they shall cast out devils, they shall speak with new tongues . . . they shall lay hands upon the sick and they shall recover.'"

Suddenly, the same voice that had spoken to him that morning spoke to him again. "It said, 'Bob, there's a woman out there tonight who's blind and I want to restore her sight.' I thought, *'What?'* But it was so real I told them that I believed there was a woman out there who was blind and God wanted to restore her sight." A female way in the back corner of the mission raised her hand. Bob said he was "scared stiff" but told her to come forward, that if she believed she could be healed. When she agreed, Rice reached out, touched the woman on the forehead, and said, "In the Name of Jesus, receive your sight!"

"The next thing I knew, the lady was laying on the floor," recounted the burly former truck driver. "I said, 'Oh, my God, what have I done now.' I had never seen anyone rest in the Spirit. It was the first time. A few seconds later, she started to cry out, 'I can see! I can see!' Then the same voice spoke to me again and said there was a man who was deaf in his left ear. I saw what happened the first time and decided to try it again. Boom. He was laying on the floor. Here this guy is laying on the floor and he got up a few minutes later and he had his hearing!"

Lastly was a woman whose hands and knuckles were gnarled with arthritis.

"The Lord told me to have her stand there with hands raised where everyone could see her hands and to praise Him, and that's what I told her to do. As she started to praise Him, we saw her hands just open up and those knots on her knuckles just dissolve before her eyes. That's how my healing ministry was launched thirty-seven years ago."

But that was hardly the end of the story.

Rice became a pastor—taking over a "church" with only three members. "I started finding everything I could in the Bible and preached healing, healing, healing, healing—and every time I preached, somebody got healed," he recalled. "It wasn't long before I was knocking walls out to accommodate the crowds." There were first dozens, then hundreds, of alleged cures. "I started operating in the gifts of the Spirit and didn't even know there were gifts of the Spirit!" he said—recalling another case in which a man had terminal lung cancer and only three weeks to live. He had been given special permission for release from the hospital to attend the healing service. "We went ahead and prayed for him and it felt like the Lord touched him," said Bob. "As soon as it was over, he had to go back to the hospital. But three weeks later, he came to the church again to testify that the morning [after the healing service], they had run some tests on him and could not find a trace of that cancer. It was gone." Rice said the Lord spoke to him *again* and told him the man was missing a rib. "I asked him why he was missing a rib, and he told me that when the doctors worked on him, they took the rib out because they had to take the lung out and put it back in. But the rib, they couldn't put back. We prayed for him again and he felt this tremendous burning going around his chest. He came back several weeks later with a set-up of before and after x-rays. God had put that rib back in that man's chest."

(The claims are extraordinary—even by the standards of those in the healing ministry. I submit them for your discernment. In all, Rice started six different churches. He described himself as an independent charismatic preacher. In 1994 his first wife died, and Rice, who by now was in the state of Washington, moved to Arizona to be near a son. There he met a Catholic woman and remarried. The members of a new church he pastored resisted the fact that his wife was an "unsaved" Catholic, and Dr. Rice decided to leave the church and become a Catholic himself—"one of *them*.")

18

Body and spirit

'Do you not know that your bodies are members of Christ?' (I Corinthians 6:15).

Ill health is turbulence. Live in His naturalness, despite our artificial world (which, to our regret, lives in *us*). Look around and note the many residues that come from everywhere in our environment: The plastic in computers. The silicone in cell phones. The electromagnetism from wi-fi and microwaves and cordless phones and digital clocks—or electric blankets. Bluetooth. CAT scans. Television. Some kids put cell phones under their pillows at night!—sleeping with microwaves—and we are all in contact not just with radiation but with synthetic materials that leach their way into us. When obese people lose weight too rapidly in highly industrialized areas, the toxic chemicals stored in their fat are released and in some cases have caused effects. Our fat is poisonous, and so are chemical traces to be found in human mother's milk. This is not God's Plan. A large number of chronic ailments get back to the way we have divorced ourselves from His Creation.

It's true that we live longer than humans did a hundred years ago, but that's due largely to vaccines (some of which are indeed lifesavers, others not) and antibiotics. Longevity comes at hospitals that are better equipped, that use MRIs to see inside the body, that handle a heart attack such that it is no longer the death knell. We have medicine to pump into the heart. We have defibrillators. We replace valves. It's why there are so many accounts of the other side: medical science has brought millions back from the "dead"; what technicians can do is wondrous. To imagine that one day surgery would be accomplished through laparoscopy—a small illuminated tube—or that blocked arteries could be restored by inserting a thin tube into a *leg*, or that every part of the eye could be treated surgically, would have been too impossible to believe a few decades ago. We reattach limbs. Irises are sewn together. Epidemics are averted. (Remember polio, mumps, chicken pox, and measles?) The list of problems that can be managed and defeated through pharmaceuticals and surgery is staggering. (If there is a problem, there is medication for it.) The exploration of space opened new vistas by creating advanced technologies that along with new chemicals have found a medical application. There is digital imaging of the breast. There are tiny transmitters that monitor a baby in the womb. There are light-emitting diodes to aid in surgeries deep in the brain—some of which are now done with the person awake and even speaking during the surgery to loved ones! There is insulin. How many times have you wondered with awe (and nearly reverence) over all the aches that are now addressed by taking a pill?

But that word "reverence" is a sticking point: we are to revere God only. And often modern medicine comes down to living longer than we did a century ago but dying uglier; for all we know, many centuries ago people lived longer than we do now, but *without* the technology. Did they count years differently back then? Isaac married Rebekah at age "forty," became a father of twins at age "sixty," and was one hundred when Esau was married. (He died, it was said, at "180.") In our time are those Hunzas who—some claim—live to be 120 or even up to 140 (and do not die connected to tubes after long months or years of disability from arthritis, blood sugar, poor eyesight, artery blockages, dementia, strokes, or tumors.)

Whatever the credibility of age numbers, it emphasizes the point of going first with what God created—His "technology." This is the vehicle to health, when coupled with spirituality and necessary medical assistance (and medicine often is needed). When we leave God out—replace Him with inventions—the result can be cancerous. It's a universal rule: circumvent God and there is a price to pay. We will never outsmart Him. We will never even be able to comprehend His intelligence. We have no clue as to how He can be Who He is. He is far too large. He is far too great. He has no limits. The very word "intelligence" is vastly too inadequate for Him. He operates across this universe and countless dimensions. Those dimensions (and universes and worlds within them and societies within those) are in concert only when they are in concert with His Spirit.

The key to good health is thus praying to Him every morning, before we set out: what our bodies need for us to eat; what we must avoid; our inner purity (which heals).

As one expert (a physician) wrote, "Jesus ate primarily natural foods in their natural states—lots of vegetables, especially beans, and lentils. He would have eaten wheat bread, fruit, drunk a lot of water and also red wine. And He would only eat meat on special occasions, maybe once a month." Grapes. Barley. Lettuce. Parsley. Basil. Lettuce. Horseradish. Peppers. Endive. Apples. Apricots. Melons. Cucumbers. Fava beans. Chickpeas. Onions. Leeks.

These are all foods that surrounded the Holy Family.

A twenty-three-old identified only as "J. J." was told that he had a two percent chance of living out the year due to cancer that had spread from a testicle to his lungs, left kidney, and neck. Desperate doctors tried intravenous chemotherapy, which led to racking convulsions.

"[One] night, he dreamed his (deceased) mother came to him and told him, 'Go to St. Joseph's Oratory' in Montreal,'" wrote author William Fischer in a book called *How to Fight Cancer and Win.* So compelling was the dream that J. J. climbed the many steps to the oratory on his knees. Soon after, he heard about the strict and simple diet of macrobiotics, whereby foods, especially whole grains, are eaten in their natural state, though he didn't try it right away. Meanwhile, the conventional treatments were wreaking havoc. J. J.'s teeth were loosening. His nausea was horrible. His mouth was encrusted with sores as the treatments destroyed much of his immune system (which should be bolstered and not compromised in order to fight cancer).

The medicine was worse than the disease, and so this young man stopped it and headed back for the oratory with his fiancée. "As J. J. made the tortuous climb up the mountain steps on his knees, he prayed at each step for his relatives, ancestors, and friend who needed help, but not for himself," noted Fischer. "J. J. grew up with a strong belief that God knows what you need; you don't have to ask. With each step up, he experienced a warm feeling, [in thinking] that he would practice macrobiotics, the tumors would disappear, and he would regain his health. *And so it happened.* When the young couple returned home, they began studying macrobiotics and put the program into practice. Once he began the macrobiotic diet, J. J. saw his strength return quickly. After a year, blood tests showed no signs of cancer and the tumor in his neck had virtually disappeared. His wasted body was fleshed out with healthy muscle, his hair had grown back, and he was once again trim and fit. A very vital young man, J. J. himself says he feels better now than when he was playing high-school football."

19

Wonderful harmony

'Let us draw near with a sincere heart in full assurance of faith, having our hearts sprinkled clean from an evil conscience and our bodies washed with pure water' (Hebrews 10:22)

Closeness with the earth (but not earth worship!) and its potential to heal was perhaps demonstrated by Jesus when (*John* 9:6-7) "He spat on the ground, and made clay of the spittle, and applied the clay to [the blind man's] eyes, and said to him, *'Go, wash in the pool of Siloam.'* So he went away and washed, and came back seeing." Herbs, which have been used by every ancient civilization, are mentioned in the Book of Genesis (1:29), where God says He has given us "every herb bearing seed"—and mentioned also in the last book of the Bible, *Revelation* (22:2), where it says that the leaves of fruit trees are "for the healing of the nations." In *Exodus* the Lord tells Moses to take "sweet spices, stacte, and onycha, and galbanum." In *Isaiah* (38:21) the prophet says to "take a lump of figs, and lay it for a plaster upon the boil, and he shall recover."

In the Book of Solomon, spikenard, saffron, calamus, and cinnamon, along with "frankincense, myrrh, and aloes" are mentioned. Though we must always be on guard against those who promote herbs from the standpoint of paganism (New Age), it is curious that the crown of thorns placed on Our Lord is thought by many to have been from a hawthorn bush and that as a herb hawthorn, according to Fischer,

107

"promotes blood circulation through the coronary arteries and serves to maintain normal blood pressure," which is also said of vinegar.

Through His wounds we are healed (*Isaiah* 53).

From *Matthew* (8:17) we know that, fulfilling Isaiah, "He took our illnesses and bore our diseases."

True health occurs on the spiritual level and your spirit will inform you as to what your body needs. Jesus will tell you.

In 1988, while residing in a poverty-stricken little town in Brazil called Rio Grande dol Sul, a Franciscan scholar named Father Romano Zago learned from local natives of a "potent all-natural recipe derived from the aloe *aborescens* plant which they used to promote supreme immune health," says the book called *Cancer—Step Outside the Box*. Father Zago began recommending it to friends and it seems that he logged remarkable results, including many healings of cancer.

Simplify. Be natural. Many foods are good for us. Because every "body" is different, we ask God what to eat and drink and the proper balance of it. Scientists get wrapped up in studies that contradict each other. Our guide is the Bible, which says: *"Behold, I have given you every plant yielding seed which is upon the face of all the earth, and every tree with seed in its fruit" (Genesis* 1:29*). "You shall have them all for food."*

Consult the Holy Spirit. (Milk and yogurt are not for everyone.) Stay clear of foods that were genetically altered. Many "promising" and "astounding" technologies have ended up with an underside, and this is destined to be the case with crops and meat that have been fundamentally changed by humans.

The same chemical companies that gave us dioxin and PCBs are now in the business of feeding us, modifying seed (so it can take more of their herbicides), and seeking to do the same with the genes of beef, pork, fish, and poultry.

When we try to circumvent Heaven, there may seem to be a benefit—perhaps, at first, even many benefits on the surface—but down the road there is a price to pay.

Beets, tomatoes, sweet potatoes, cauliflower, eggplant, blueberries, flaxseed, Brussels sprouts, squash, avocados, and red peppers or dark green vegetables, especially broccoli, spinach, kale, dandelion, and collard greens are all very good. Nuts are important (particularly almonds, pecans, pistachios, and walnuts), as are turmeric and fish (best: salmon, sardines, and mackerel). Bad foods cause damage to the cells while good ones neutralize or repair injury caused by what are known as "free radicals," which, like rust in a pipe, are the result of exposure over time to oxidation. "Free radicals are nasty," wrote an eminent scientist, Dr. T. Colin Campbell, in a seminal, highly recommended book called *The China Study*. "They can cause our tissues to become rigid and limited in their function. It is a bit like old age, when our bodies become creaky and stiff. To a great extent, that is what aging is. This uncontrolled free-radical damage also is part of the processes that give rise to cataracts, to hardening of the arteries, to cancer, to emphysema, to arthritis and many other ailments that become common with age. *But here's the kicker*: we do not naturally build a shield to protect ourselves against free radicals. As we are not plants, we do not carry out photosynthesis and therefore do not produce any of our own anti-oxidants. Fortunately the anti-oxidants in plants work in our bodies the same way they work in plants. It is a wonderful harmony. The plants make the anti-oxidant shields, and at the same time make them look incredibly appealing with beautiful, appetizing colors. Then we animals, in turn, are attracted to the plants and eat them and borrow their antioxidant shields for our own health. Whether you believe in God, evolution, or just coincidence, you must admit that this is a beautiful, almost spiritual, example of nature's wisdom."

One of the leading food researchers in U.S. history, Dr. Campbell set forth a nutrition plan for William Clinton after the president's heart surgery and has been affiliated with institutions such at Cornell, M.I.T., and Oxford, a scientist who has received dozens of federal grants, been in line for the Nobel Prize, and has many conducted hands-on experiments, including one in China (hence the title of his book) that involved the health and diet of people in sixty-five counties there. That study, which joined other research there over the course of thirty-five years, involved not only surveys of longevity and health but blood tests on 6,500 adults, finding certain types of cancer were a hundred times lower within peasant communities in the Chinese outbacks than in modern nations such as the United States. The further away humans had gone from simplicity and naturalness, he found, the greater the chance of malignancy. It came down, again, to nutrition. They ate foods that prevent disease, containing anti-oxidants, which react with free radicals and stop the damaging chain reactions in the body.

Foods packed with antioxidants—rich, colorful foods— can help the body fight off the damage caused by inflammation. Similar results were found elsewhere. Whole grains, nuts, dark leafy greens, and fish, packed with oils and antioxidants, are a major part of the famous "Mediterranean diet," which has been shown to reduce inflammation in as little as six weeks, a diet popular in the less modern parts of Greece, Spain, Croatia, and Italy.

While all of us have cancerous cells in our bodies, a strong immune system, bolstered by anti-oxidants, rids the body of malignant cells, at the same time helping our immune system neutralize free radicals.

Dr. Campbell and his team found that the death rate from coronary heart disease was *seventeen times higher* among American men than rural Chinese!

The U.S. death rate from breast cancer—meanwhile—was five times higher than in rural China.

During one three-year period of observation, Dr. Campbell reports that "not one single person died of coronary heart disease before the age of sixty-four" among 427,000 men surveyed in the provinces of Sichuan and Guizhou.

A lot of it goes back to what we all know about: cholesterol.

What Dr. Campbell and his researchers learned was not only that cholesterol clogs arteries, connected as it is to inflammation, but causes cancer as well.

As blood-cholesterol levels decreased in blood samples, so did the prevalence, among those tested, of colon, liver, rectal, lung, breast, blood, brain, stomach, and esophageal tumors.

Intake of meat and dairy were associated with higher rates, and eating plant-based meals was clearly linked to lower ones.

God gives us a free will to choose.

Diets heavy on meat were most associated with female health issues: menstruation, late menopause, and most seriously, breast cancer.

Yet (more remarkably still), Dr. Campbell and his researchers learned during these and other surveys (in India, the Philippines, and the U.S. itself) that a shift in diet could *turn* cancer off like a switch. The key was reducing animal protein.

As he put it, "Nutrients from animal-based foods increased tumor development while nutrients from plant-based foods decreased tumor development."

Such a decrease was especially noted with those colorful vegetables. The purple in eggplant, that red in tomatoes, and the lush deep green in leafy vegetables have been designed by God to attract us. (If we are to eat meat, it should be with fruits and vegetables.) Like the soul, those must be in balance. Currently the most prevalent "vegetable" in the modern diet is French fries.

A diet strong in anti-oxidants can even negate the effects of carcinogens.

It can stop free radicals from binding to our DNA.

A study by another scientist of eighteen people who had suffered serious and often repeated coronary attacks and then were placed on a strict vegetarian diet found just *one* suffered a heart event in the following eleven years.

Milk is what Dr. Campbell (who grew up on a dairy farm, only to eschew it) calls "an exceptionally potent cancer promoter" (others disagree). Yet, high protein levels from vegetables had no such negative effect—rather, as I said, negated such effects. At the end of two years, all the animals fed high levels of animal protein in yet another study were dead or near death from liver tumors while all animals fed low levels of animal protein were alive. The same kind of things were seen in studying the diets and diseases of people in the Philippines and India. Human mother's milk is one thing. Our consumption, however, of cow milk—especially in that it also brings along artificial hormones pumped into cows—may be another. Did God intend for humans to drink the milk of other animals?

Is it in the plan of nature for a youngster to rely so heavily on milk after nursing years?

Through major change in diet, scientific journals have reported that diabetic patients can often go off their medication, that heart disease can be reversed, that breast cancer can be controlled or outright eliminated, that mental performance improves (perhaps preventing dementia, including Alzheimer's), and that less deadly but painful conditions such as arthritis and kidney stones can in part be prevented. Joining nutrition to spiritual recourse (and medical assistance) brings the best outcome.

For we see that what causes minor problems like allergies can be early warnings.

In His design the Lord has structured biology such that what causes sleep disorders, stomach acid, psoriasis, or headaches may also be implicated in more serious potential disorders (such as heart problems). There are many examples.

The next time you're at the supermarket, remember that the majority of products in the middle aisles (that vast region between coolers) are laden with unhealthy preservatives, dyes, salt, and trans-fats (though this will soon be outlawed, and are in pastries, margarine, shortening, frosting, nondairy creamers, microwave popcorn, cookies, biscuits and rolls, donuts, crackers, and frozen dinners, to name a few more, but not all), sugars, or artificial colors, as are many items in those coolers, especially processed cold cuts.

If you have to have sugar, perhaps go for cane sugar that's organic. Stay clear of most chips. Flee from the soda counters. (And remember: the first ingredients listed on a label are usually the ones in greatest quantity.)

Now let's look again at substances that may reverse problems caused by incorrect eating and lead to *cures*.

When it comes to cancer, remarkable recoveries have been associated not only with a vegetable diet, good water, and exercise but also with more exotic things like flaxseed oil (emphasize this), apricot kernels (which the Hunzas insist are the key to their longevity), co-enzyme Q-10 (a very important compound), Essiac tea, vitamins C and D, the aloe I have mentioned, and particularly foods that lower the acidity of your blood (raising the "pH" or alkalinity).

Cancer doesn't like a neutral or alkaline environment, nor one rich in oxygen. I spoke to an Irishman who was close to Padre Pio's inner circle and said the priest had once prophesied that *"there will be a cure for cancer, and it will be so simple the medical experts will all wonder why they never thought of it earlier."* (When I prayed about this, the word "alkaline" popped into my mind. Looking it up on the internet, I noticed, to my surprise, that many claim alkaline foods ward off cancer formation.) "In the 1930s, an interesting natural cancer treatment was proposed as a simple, effective answer to cancer—almost any cancer," said one website. "This treatment approach is not well known because it is considered alternative or experimental—or even dangerous—by the medical and scientific community and hence has been referenced primarily in obscure publications outside the mainstream press. This treatment approach is called alkaline therapy or pH therapy and is based in part on observations of cultures without significant incidence of cancer and in part on scientific observations of and experimentation with cellular metabolism. The principles of pH therapy are very simple. The metabolism of cancer cells has a very narrow pH tolerance for cellular proliferation (mitosis), which is between 6.5 and 7.5. As such, if you can interfere with cancer cell metabolism by either lowering or raising the internal cancer cell pH, you can theoretically stop cancer progression."

You may want to look up lists of alkaline foods and even buy saliva strips that tell you if your system is acidic or at a proper pH. Garlic, onions, apple-cider vinegar, almonds, pumpkin seeds, bananas, carrots, spinach, lemons, apples, and avocados are examples.

"I am a very well-informed lay person on the subject after several decades of investigation," a viewer of our website, Donna Sherwood of Brooklyn, wrote me. "I have looked over any number of alternative approaches to treatment and cure of cancer. I cannot think of one which does not have at its core the restoration of pH balance along an alkaline rating. Food is key and elimination of all foods which create acidic *habitus* is critical. Unfortunately this is made especially difficult due to agricultural practices in the U.S. since the Sixties. Fruit, if not vine-ripened, will never transition to an alkaline state. Most alternative food recommendations contain minimum amounts of fruits due to belief that cancer cells feed off sugar. Fruits would be neutral if they were allowed to ripen naturally. 'Slash, burn and toxify' is not an effective nor humane treatment for organic disease. There are many different protocols which effectively treat and reverse cancer and our medical establishment is actively persecuting those pursuing them, both patients and practitioners. I cannot tell you the remarks I have heard from these [specialists] to fourth-stage patients who they have failed but still discouraging them about looking to other sources! I personally know many people given prognosis of imminent death who walked away and became well."

20

Light comes through surrender

'In Him was life, and the life was the Light of men' (John 1:4)

Many are the pieces to the puzzle, and mixed is the dietary counsel. In the end it is God's Love and direction that make us whole.

When we deprive ourselves—not nutritionally, but of carnality— we're in touch with eternity (transcending the flesh); and when we're in touch with Heaven we are in touch with the potential to heal ourselves and others. What did the Lord say when His disciples could not cast out a spirit that had dragged a boy into lunacy? *"This kind does not go out except by prayer and fasting" (Matthew 17: 18-21).* In the same passage He said that faith can move a "mountain." He was not speaking about Everest, but of darkness. Writes deliverance expert K. A. Schneider, "When we choose not to follow the easy path of giving in to the flesh, but deny ourselves in order to receive more of Him, we will be nourished by the Holy Spirit and built up in our faith in Jesus."

I spoke to a Catholic man named Lawrence Leonard from Hillsboro, Missouri, who suffered heart attacks at the young ages of thirty-one and thirty-four and was ready to go for a catheterization at St. Louis University Hospital. Before that, however, he attended a Full Gospel dinner where the speaker was a Christian television commentator who often called out descriptions of those who would be healed (as we saw too with Bob Rice).

"I was sitting in the back, listening to him, and he said there would be miracles that night," recalled Leonard, who was very skeptical at first but had a mustard seed of faith. "I believed in miracles but had never seen one. He said there would be a miracle over cancer, etcetera, and called out descriptions and had people stand up. Then he said, 'There's a young man who has heart trouble.' I said to myself, 'so what; there's a thousand people here. There's probably twenty-five men with heart troubles.' Two or three stood up, but the speaker said they weren't the ones. He said the man was wearing a blue suit. I was still skeptical. People either wear blue or black suits, I said to myself. Another guy stood up and [the speaker] said, 'No, you're not the one.' Then he described the color of the shirt the man was wearing. It was mine, but I still thought, 'It's not me.' I didn't think I was worthy. Besides, I was a Catholic at a Protestant dinner. Those with me wanted me to stand up but I wouldn't. Then he described my tie but I still wouldn't stand up. Then he pointed to my part of the room and when I looked he was pointing *straight at me!*"

For several days after, says Lawrence, he could feel "something going on with my chest." The catheterization was still scheduled, and a week or so after the dinner he went for an preparatory examination.

The examination showed that there was no heart damage.

No longer were there signs that he'd had two heart attacks.

"They said they couldn't explain what had happened," related Lawrence, a businessman who owned a construction company and now manages commercial properties; three decades later he has no coronary illness.

Healing by faith and food is sometimes sullied by those who exaggerate. At the convention center in New York City, I watched a well-known Evangelical healer causing many to spring up from their wheelchairs as he barked ailments in the microphone and asked for donations. There was little question that folks were springing out of wheelchairs. But there was no way of knowing how badly these people had needed a wheelchair to start with nor how long the "healing" would last (for if an evil spirit has caused an illness, the demon, in theory, can also remove it. It is why one always prays first. A demon can cause temporary cures that may eventually lead a person into a worst state, perhaps even new ailments.) What are we to make of a Christian doctor who points in church at a boy's tumor after which it vanishes? Or causes a "pop" that signals detachment of a growth on a crucial facial nerve in a nun? Or makes a curved spine to reshape like putty (but also, in private practice, uses a type of acupuncture based on electricity)? It is hard to say. (He had the support of a bishop.)

But we can know that with discipline we're operating on all cylinders, purging impurities (moving mountains, or at least hills) and expanding our trust. There is the case of Therese Daoud, who went to Ichilov Hospital in Tel Aviv with a huge tumor in her leg. The only option, doctors told her (according to *Israel Today*), was amputation. But after three attempts at going for the drastic surgery, each delayed for various reasons, Therese decided that this was a sign to pray, which she did in earnest, and the next time she went to see her doctor, the tumor—once the size of an orange— had dramatically receded and was no longer cancerous. When her doctor had asked her what she'd been doing, she explained that she had been praying. ("If someone had told me the story of what happened to Therese, I would have said they are crazy and sent them to a mental hospital," said Professor Yaakov Bickels, head of the hospital's oncology department. "But I saw it with my own eyes.")

It's when we stray into healing apart from the Lord— and begin to idolize a healer, or go for laying-on-of-the-hands without prayer and fasting—that the pursuit of a miracle can be questionable. Out there are occultists, shamans, false Christian healers, Reiki masters, practitioners of hypnosis, experts on therapeutic touch, New Agers, and psychic "healers." (I met one who told me he got his start when God communicated to him Morse-code-like by causing his car locks to click up and down.)

Yet when it is done in the Name of Jesus, after discernment, we think of the passage in *Matthew* 12: "When the Pharisees heard *this*, they said, 'This man casts out demons only by Beelzebul the ruler of the demons.' And knowing their thoughts Jesus said to them, 'Any kingdom divided against itself is laid waste; and any city or house divided against itself will not stand. If Satan casts out Satan, he is divided against himself; how then will his kingdom stand? If I by Beelzebul cast out demons, by whom do your sons cast *them* out? For this reason they will be your judges. But if I cast out demons by the Spirit of God, then the kingdom of God has come upon you'" (24-28).

His Power is our life and it is our true existence; we are most open to healing when we spread kindness. The heart must be open. It is the channel of Grace. The mind must be focused on Him. Fear is a stumbling block. The Light of life comes through surrender. Hand your illness to Jesus on the Crucifix. If your suffering is redemptive, that's free will (a choice) or perhaps it is not redemptive suffering. MacNutt argued that the cross Jesus carried was the cross of persecution, the kind of suffering that comes from the outside because of evil. The suffering that Jesus was *not* recorded as having endured during His Life but rather the kind of suffering He took *away* from those who approached Him was that of *sickness*. Wrong emotions cause wrong eating and lead to ailments. The old expression calls anger "bad bile." A "nervous wreck" wrecks organs. Bitterness is the taste of poison. For all we know, "beating our brains out"— anxiety—may contribute to aneurisms. If we are emotionally "bent out of shape" perhaps we are more prone to bone disorders. Foods "to die for" may lead, eventually, in old age, to just that. Something that "turns the stomach" could lead to an ulcer (if we let it). And then there are the spiritual forces Dr. McAll spoke about.

When Christ spoke of "unclean" spirits, was this the same as when He mentioned the word "ghost" (as differentiated from demon)? If there are spirits around that are unclean, and if we are not properly sealed, if there are access points, we might be susceptible to their uncleanness in the same use of this word as was employed in Jesus' time for the "uncleanness" of lepers. We energize such forces with fear, and there are those who believe that souls of the deceased who linger in an earthly limbo out of accordance with the Will of God can transmit whatever diseases they harbored, or at least the darkness that caused affliction. A Christian columnist named Bryan Fischer notes that Jesus seemed to make a distinction between physical and demonic illnesses, casting out demons with words in the case of evil but laying on His Hands when the ailment was physical. In cases where a healing does not occur, it may be because God has a higher purpose. There can be a multitude of spirits. All darkness should be commanded away from us in the Name of Jesus on a daily basis. Mysterious illnesses are often rooted in mysterious sources out of reach for medical technicians. Souls who are earthbound are often this way out of a confusion or fear that they can then transmit. We are drained of energy. It is not always the weather. Ill will is a will that causes illness. The remedy is a personal relationship with Jesus. He must be in our midst, your closest friend. Never obsess over the deceased. It is the enemy who causes depression, despair, distress, and pessimism. Health leaves when strength does. "Since we all have cancer cells floating around in our bodies, the key to health is strengthening what happens in our spirit to activate our immune systems," said MacNutt. Loneliness and lack of love depress our immune system and our desire to love, he taught. Loners tend to develop cancer and anger increases our proneness to heart disease, he said. As a lonely and sick woman told another author, "I had an empty place in me and cancer grew to fill it." A healing priest named Father Lou Cerulli, of Montreal, believes there are just too many cases where recurring problems, such as divorce, alcoholism, financial problems, accidents, run in families. When a person dies, he believes, spirits that caused such problems or spiritual proclivities are passed on to the descendants. "All of us are affected at least to some degree," Father Cerulli said. "Some people are more affected than others. Some people have no problems until they are forty or fifty. There are always degrees. But if you're going back to all the generations, there is going to be something. Whether we're aware of it or not is another question."

Create the environment of health and you and your loved ones will be healthy.

Fill your home with prayer that goes directly to Jesus.

"One of the greatest losses the Church has suffered has been her disbelief in the full heritage of healing power," notes Dr. MacNutt, who points out that half of the passages in the first eight chapters of *Mark* deal with healing.

An electrician in Butte, Montana, Bob O'Bill, promised God in 1979 that he would erect a life-sized statue of the

Virgin Mary if his wife recovered from serious cancer. She did and Bob erected not a life-sized statue but the tallest of Mary in the country, placing it on the jagged Rocky Mountain Continental Divide three thousand feet above Butte.

Miraculously, Mrs. O'Bill had made a complete recovery.

It is the sanctity, aroma, and song of Heaven—the healthiness of Godliness—that we must tap: living waters, the atmosphere of radiant grass, the lakes that capture a molten golden glow of the sky, the aroma of violets and lilies (but so much better) that soothes the spirit. In Heaven music heals like thousands of choir songs all joined as one in perfect angelic unison with the penetration of a trumpet but also the glide and sweet soothing pitch of a flute or violin.

Tap into this.

A diver named Ian described the luminosity after a brush with death from a deadly box jellyfish off the coast of Mauritius. "As I stepped into the light," he said, "it was as if I'd come inside veils of suspended shimmering lights, like suspended stars or diamonds giving off the most amazing radiance. And as I walked through the light it continued to heal the deepest part of me, it was healing my broken inner man, wonderfully healing my broken heart. I aimed for the brightest part of the light. Standing in the center of the light stood a Man with dazzling white robes reaching down to his bare feet. The garments were not man-made fabrics but were like garments of light. As I lifted my eyes up I could see the chest of a Man with His arms outstretched as if to welcome me. I looked towards His face. It was so bright; it seemed to be about ten times brighter than the light I'd already seen. It made the sun look yellow and pale in comparison. It was so bright that I couldn't make out the features of His face, and as I stood there I began to sense that the light was emitting purity and holiness. I knew I was standing in the Presence of Almighty God—no one but God could look like this. The purity and holiness continued to come forth from His face and I began to feel that purity and holiness enter into me."

When RaNelle Wallace, burned in that horrible crash, saw eternity, she found herself, to recap, in a light that was "like a nuclear explosion. The light pierced me. Every particle of me was shot through with blinding, brilliant light, and I had a feeling of transparency. My skin didn't burn. My eyes still saw. I floated in this light, bathed in it, and the love that surrounded me and filled me was sweeter and finer than anything I had ever felt. I was changed by it, refined, rarefied, made pure. I basked in its sweetness, and the traumas of the past were far behind me, forgotten and transformed by peace. My hand was clear, like transparent gel, but there was light coursing through it like clear blood. The light didn't run in irregular patterns as it would in veins; rather, it shot right through my hands like rays or beams. My whole hand sparkled with light. And I noticed again that they weren't burned. My feet and hands were perfect and whole. They radiated this glistening, beaming light."

This is the true you and when directed by God it heals the body on earth.

The transmission of health is from the "glorified being."

Light is life.

"Around three p.m., after having prayed the Chaplet of Divine Mercy, we walked back to our lodging, where an irresistible force drew me to look towards Mount Krizevac [a holy mountain of prayer]," said a pilgrim who was healed of a chronic blood flow from severe kidney problems. "There I saw a blinding light at the foot of the Cross. The light kept getting bigger and bigger and, within it, I saw a figure like Our Lady: it moved from left to right, but kept coming back to the foot of the Cross. I understood then that this supernatural light was active; it had penetrated each cell of my body, all of my being. Less than an hour later, I found that the blood had disappeared from my urine."

"When something comes from God, you have harmony, great joy, and a great peace," said seer Vicka Ivankovic Matovic there. "You can't feel well if you have fear in your heart. When you feel fear, confusion, and anguish, it comes from the enemy. You can't trust your feelings if you do not have inner harmony. For sure, suffering cannot be explained; it can only be lived in one's own heart. When the Lord gives us a suffering—a cross, pain—this is really a big gift. We often think, how can sickness be a gift? But it's a big gift! Only God knows why He gives this gift and only He knows the reason for when He takes it back. It is only up to us how we are ready to accept this. It is enough to say, 'Thank you God for this gift, that you still have something that you want to give to me, I am ready to receive it. I ask only your strength and courage so that I may carry on.' And also the Madonna has told us, 'you don't know how great is the value of your suffering in the eyes of God.' There are different kinds of suffering: there is the suffering that God gives and there is the suffering that we make for ourselves, and these are two different things, they don't have the same value. We must try to accept that which the Lord wants and we must give thanks and when one gives thanks for this great gift, then graces and fruits and everything come sooner. And then we can't say 'I'm suffering, I'm in pain,' God knows this: accept it, don't talk about it. One who is still able to speak isn't suffering. Suffering is to be lived in our souls and in our hearts. God is always ready to give healing. But for God it's not so easy for him to give us this gift because there are problems. What are these problems? It is like this: many times when there is some difficulty or suffering for our children, a husband, or one of our neighbors, we beg God with great energy to heal their suffering;

we are ready to accept anything, do everything, get on our knees, pray for hours but only for that particular moment. The Madonna is ready to give the grace that is being requested. And many times the grace is given in order to show that person that God is near. But the Madonna also said that those graces are not to be played around with, because the Madonna said that after receiving a miracle, some people behave worse than before and then the next time they need a special grace, they pray expecting to be satisfied a second time; they think, 'You gave me [a healing] once before so must give me [a healing] again today.' In this way we start playing around with these graces from God. Already the Madonna said to us, *'there is no problem for graces; I am able to give them; through my Son I can pray for these gifts and give them; but the problem is with your hearts. You all ask for healing of everything in the body, but too few ask for healing of the heart. When your hearts begin to heal,* then your bodies will begin to heal.' We must pray to have a lively faith. We should pray every day for this gift and this gift will grow every day in our hearts."

A woman from northeastern Florida sent me a note saying, "I wrote a couple of years ago to say that our middle son, Andrew, had fallen ill with vaccine-induced autism. I believe that Our Lord is asking me to share the follow-up story with you: It has become so clear to me, through hindsight and the Holy Spirit, why this had to happen to Andrew.

"My son, like all of the children with vaccine-induced autism, are little messengers of God. They are angels on a mission to teach us that we must turn back to God and to a more natural way of living that is in accordance with God's creation, as opposed to a chemical/synthetic world such as the one we are creating through science and medicine. When Andrew was about four weeks old, I went to lay down and, as soon as my head touched the pillow, I had a vision – not a dream, but a vision. It was so real. I saw my baby lying in his crib. And kneeling beside the crib, praying, was a male angel dressed in a brown robe with a gold-colored rope for a sash, the kind the Franciscans wear. And I heard Our Lady's voice say, *'Spend every moment you can with him.'* Then the vision ended. I sat bolt upright in the bed and thought that I was being prepared for my child to die. I got on my knees and begged God not to take him. But I remembered, also, the promise I had made in Adoration [of giving and trusting my children to Jesus, at His request], and asked that Our Lord would give me the strength to bear whatever His Will would be for Andrew's life. Weeks later, I told my mother and sister about the vision; I was still so shaken by it. When I took my son for his twelve-month-old check-up, I asked the pediatrician which vaccine he was to receive. I was told it was the MMR (Measles-Mumps-Rubella). I told the doctor that I had read an article just the week before (I think on *Spirit Daily*), that said the MMR, along with twelve other vaccines, was cultured on the cell lines of aborted fetuses. I explained to the pediatrician that, as a pro-life Catholic, I would object to and refuse that particular vaccine based on my moral and religious beliefs. The doctor became furious at this claim and said it was 'a lie made up by extremists on the right who have an agenda to push.' He stormed out of the office and returned with the package insert. He unrolled it in front of me like a scroll and said, 'Here. Look at this and tell me where it says aborted fetuses were used!'

"I was shocked by his reaction, but I also had nothing more to go on than the one article, and I couldn't even remember the source. I felt silly and unsure, so I went along and allowed Andrew to be immunized with the MMR. I later found out that, indeed, the vaccine is created using cell lines from aborted fetuses. The week before my son was diagnosed with autism, I went for a walk on the beach. I stopped to pick up a bird feather. Again I heard a voice. This time it said, *'Hope is a prayer with wings.'* Later that day, I was at the bookstore. As I walked past rows of books toward the checkout, I spotted one whose title read *H.O.P.E.* It was a book about digestive health and how to heal the gut. I bought it on a hunch. Later, it became invaluable in understanding and healing my child's 'leaky gut syndrome,' another aspect of autism. The day Andrew was first diagnosed with autism, he had just turned two. I was reeling from shock, disbelief, and confusion. *What had happened to my precious, healthy child? How could this be?* I remembered again that I had committed my children to the care and protection of Our Lord.

"That night, I read Andrew a bedtime story and tried not to break down in tears until I had put him to bed. I knew at that moment that Jesus was right there with me and, just as in the poem 'Footprints,' He was going to carry my family through this. I kept thinking, *'You have to persevere in hope. Do not give up hope for even one instant.'* I have witnessed the special connection that children with autism have to Jesus and Our Blessed Mother. When Andrew was two and a half and completely nonverbal, he took my agnostic sister, who struggles with infertility, by the hand and led her into the Shrine of Our Lady of Le Leche that bears a statue of Our Lady holding the Infant Jesus (in St. Augustine, Florida). Andrew motioned for her to kneel down. Then, without words, he invited her to clasp her hands and bow her head in prayer. It was a beautiful scene to watch! At three years old, Andrew had few words but such incredible comprehension that the speech pathologist recommended he get a handheld computer device to speak for him. Our insurance company agreed to pay for the device. Around the same time, we met a biomedical doctor who was willing to run the blood tests that my husband and I had been asking for.

"The tests came back showing conclusively that Andrew had been infected with measles and rubella. The tests also showed that our son's immune system was barely functional – because his little body, by that time, had been fighting these viruses for nearly two years, which led to an auto-immune disorder. We began using vitamin supplements and B12 shots to get his immune system functioning again. We also switched to a gluten-and-casein free diet and went organic as much as possible. We used homeopathy to detox his body from the viruses and heavy metals and to heal the damage that had been done. Within weeks of detoxing Andrew from the damage his vaccines had caused, he began speaking and behaving more normally. When I called the lady at the insurance company to say that we would not need the speaking device after all, she said that she had never heard of a patient recovering to the point of not needing a speaking device, especially in only a few months time! More important than all of the physical remedies: I not only prayed for my son but over my son. I asked for the intercession of so many saints, especially Our Blessed Mother. For example I asked St. John Chrysostom, the saint with the 'golden voice,' to pray for Andrew's voice to be restored. I stood on the Scripture in *Mark* where Jesus healed the deaf and mute man when He said, *'Ephatha!'* that is, 'Be opened!' I claimed the Scriptures for my child. I anointed his forehead with Holy Water and blessed oil daily as I prayed over him. And perhaps most powerful of all, I praised God and thanked Him every day for Andrew's healing long before he was actually healed. I also prayed every day that I would be given the grace to hope beyond hope and never lose faith that my child would be healed.

"Indeed, Andrew has been healed of autism! All praise and glory be to God! He goes to school with normally developing children, and people are shocked when I tell them that he has recovered from autism. He is now a normal, active four-year-old. When he was finally able to speak (which he now does in full sentences), Andrew said, 'Mommy, Jesus is the Bible.' I said, 'Yes, much of the Bible is about Jesus.' To which he replied, 'No. Jesus is the Bible, Mommy.' I encountered another autistic boy at the doctor's office one day. He looked to be twelve or thirteen but had the social skills and speech of a five-year-old. I asked him if he liked to swim. He said yes. I asked if he liked to swim in the pool or the ocean. And he replied, 'Ma'am, I don't have an ocean, but I have a river, and His Name is Jesus.' These kids are so close to Our Lord! I believe that God allowed this to happen to Andrew. I have met literally hundreds of parents with the same or a similar story to Andrew's, and they have found renewed hope that their child can recover. This experience has also opened my eyes to the many ways our children are being harmed through vaccines. I know the vaccine issue is just one of many sins against God and His Creation. Our bodies are His temple, Scripture says. The Bible also says that 'we perish for lack of knowledge'" (*Proverbs* 10:21).

21

With prayer you are never alone

'The Lord will rescue me from every evil deed,' (II Timothy 4:18)

Thus does the Light from Christ instruct us. Sometimes, it seems trivial—we look for the spectacular. Often, He nudges us on how to live and eat.

"An apple a day may help keep the doctor away, but if you add a carrot a day he'll probably stay away!" writes a priest. "The carrot is the king of the vegetables. It is loaded with vitamin A which helps your immune system."

We choose (free choice) our emotions.

"We let jealousy invade us," said another priest. "It torments us and turns into an actual illness. We start saying bad things and making negative comments."

We are blinded not by the light but by the will—warned when we lack peace.

"Do you know how we lose peace?" asked this same priest. "When we begin to see only one aspect of a person, an aspect that we don't like, ignoring the whole person." Then criticism enters. By focusing on the one thing that upsets us, we are blinded. We lose sight of the beauty in the person. When we lose sight of that, we lose love for the person and there is that much less total love within us. When it leaves, it leaves a void where illness finds roost. Wrong thoughts "eat away" at us—rot the flesh, the bones. If you do not forgive others (and yourself), you can be held back from healing.

See Jesus walking through your life as He walked through Galilee, as He walked through the Gadarenes, and let Him lay His Hands on what ails you most—the deep wounds to which demons can attach.

Evil cannot grasp love nor inhabit a place in us that is filled with it.

Says the Lord, do not bind to the condemnation of the devil (always look for that bright place beyond).

Do you think God is always trying to throw a curse at you, to trip you up or hurt you? Do you always feel like you are on His "bad side"? Healing is essential to the message of Jesus and carries us all the way back to the very idea of Him. When there is a physical cause for an infirmity, a physical cure should be sought, along with prayer. We must hold our physicians, says *Sirach*, in a place of honor. For as it says, "he is essential to you, and God it was Who established his profession"; it is the Lord Who gives our doctors, surgeons, and technicians their wisdom. "My son," says *Sirach* (38:1-14), "delay not, but pray to God, Who will heal you: Flee wickedness; let your hands be just, cleanse your heart of every sin . . . Then give the doctor his place lest he leave; for you need him too. There are times that give him an advantage, and he too beseeches God that his diagnosis may be correct, and his treatment will bring a cure."

At the same moment, if the physician is *not* in touch with the Lord, this can lead to a spiral of unnecessary tests that cause tremendous stress: sometimes, finding things that might dissolve in time, transient cancer. This is why it is critical to pray about every step we take and go with what gives a sense of tranquility. At the doctor's office, pray for the doctor to say and do and see the right things. Pray against false diagnoses. Pray for good judgment. Pray for insight. Cast out stress. Clear the spiritual air. Take Saint

Joseph, Padre Pio, and Brother André with you. Dark thoughts and dreams are no good and can indicate attempts by the devil at affecting your energy, health, and happiness (the last he especially rejoices in taking). When you are depleted you are susceptible to sickness. What suppresses the spirit can suppress the immune system; what causes confusion can confuse the DNA; what stings the soul may also be a nettle; what darkens your eternal destination, lessening your chance of Heaven, can cast a shadow over your organs. Identify those areas that are "contaminated" and give them to God—His Wounds on the Cross. Love Him in front of the Crucifix! Go to a doctor but go first to God. Note in *2 Chronicles* 16:11-14 that King Asa contracted a serious illness and died in the forty-first year of his reign because he sought not God but only physicians. As it says (15: 2), "The Lord is with you when you are with Him, and if you seek Him He will be present to you; but if you abandon Him He will abandon you."

With prayer there is no abandonment.

A man named Jim in Dubuque, Iowa, once wrote explaining: "After losing my job, I had to go on the state public insurance plan. I am a type-2 diabetic, and am on a program that provides my insulin for free. Because of delays in getting into the new insurance, my replacement insulin was delayed and I ran into a situation where I was running out of insulin. There was going to be a week where I would not have the insulin I needed. It was available through an urgent-care facility, but I didn't have the money to buy it. With all the phone calls trying to get a source, I was desperate.

"I remembered reading about an 'express novena' that Mother Theresa would pray, called the 'Express Novena of Nine *Memorares.*' What you do is make the Sign of the Cross, state your intentions; then sincerely pray the *Memorare* prayer, state your intentions again, then pray the *Memo-*

rare and keep doing this until you have stated your intentions and recited the *Memorare* nine times. Mother Teresa really swore by the efficacy of this Express Novena of Nine *Memorares*, so I decided to try it. I prayed that I would get my insulin before I was on the new insurance—and that night I decreased my insulin injection by half. Imagine my surprise the next day when I checked and my blood sugar was at 120—in the middle of the normal range! I used the last of my insulin (about a quarter of my normal dose) and yet the next day my sugar was at 102! That was Sunday night, and my new insulin was expected to arrive on Friday. During that time, I exercised, prayed, and did what I could to eat healthy. I should note that my food stamps were also messed up, so all I had to eat was 'mac and cheese' and green beans the food bank provided. The mac and cheese should have driven up my blood sugar, but no: provided I kept up the exercise my blood sugar was well maintained (guess Mary wanted me to make sure I took care of myself!). During that time God gave me the insulin I needed, through my own body. I trusted in Him, and He provided!"

The Blessed Mother has given this prayer:

"Oh my God, behold this sick person before You. He has come to ask You what he wishes and what he considers as the most important thing for him. You, oh, my God, make these words enter into his heart: 'What is important, is the health of the soul.' Lord, may Your Will in everything take place in his regard, if You want him to be cured, let health be given to him; but if Your Will is something else, let him continue to bear his cross. I also pray to You for us, who intercede for him; purify our hearts, to make us worthy to convey Your holy Mercy. Protect him and receive his pain, that Your holy Will be done in him, that Your holy Name be revealed through him. Help him to bear his cross with courage."

She also said:

"For the cure of the sick, it is important to say the following prayers: the *Creed* and seventeen times each the *Lord's Prayer, Hail Mary,* and *Glory Be,* and to fast on bread and water. It is good to impose one's hands on the sick and to pray. It is good to anoint the sick with holy oil. All priests do not have the gift of healing. In order to receive this gift, the priest must pray with perseverance and believe firmly."

When our hearts are with God it is splendid, even if burdened with difficulties; it loses that splendor when it strays from Him.

I have my own little story from the late Eighties.

Back then I was still on the college lecture circuit and someone very close to me was found to have a lump in her breast. They planned to do a biopsy. She was very upset. The doctor was also concerned. I went to speak at a college in northern Pennsylvania, where I stayed in an apartment-style suite. Praying for this situation, I suddenly developed a high fever and started shaking all over. I was in the throes of something. I wondered if I would be able to speak that evening. I never stopped praying and the heat intensified, for quite a while excruciating. I don't know if it was five or twenty minutes. I was in deep intercession. Something caused me to simply keep praying. No doubt a Rosary was involved. I often invoke the Holy Spirit. Suddenly, it all lifted—the heat, the shivering—and a few days later when the woman went to the doctor for a check-up the physician was baffled because the lump was simply gone. I never told her what had occurred. Until now it has been a private memory.

God inspires.

A woman in the Philippines named Julie Figueroa who had "zero" chances of living due to a rare type of skull cancer was led to consume coconut oil, which many say is one of the best natural cures. "I started taking three to four tablespoons of oil a day plus whatever I used in preparing my meals," said Julie. "I would add it to my oatmeal in the morning, put it in my hot chocolate, cook my meals in it. I also snacked on fresh coconut and drank coconut juice. By July my doctors started to worry. I had been gone for nearly six months. They needed to monitor the cancer that was still in my skull. So I flew back to the U.S. To their complete surprise I had gone into remission. They asked me what I had done. I told them I found a cure—virgin coconut oil. Today I continue to use coconut oil and I am cancer free."

Others find their "miracle" in juicing carrots, lemon juice, dark greens, blueberries, or hemp seed and the list goes on: different cures for different folks, and not to be scoffed at as quackery. God provides. There is bitter melon (goya) that some believe alleviates both diabetes and pancreatic cancer.

God will lead you as to what is best for your body, guiding you to complement medical care with natural means.

Anything that bolsters the immune system or purges it is your friend.

Some believe a large number of ailments, including allergies, originate in the colon, and here I think again of figs, which have much fiber. Fiber cleanses the intestines. Apple cider vinegar can also cleanse and apple juice itself, as well as grapefruit juice, are thought to purge the liver and kidneys (in addition to providing copious vitamin C).

Many allergies originate, according to author Bruce Fife, with a *candida* infection that causes proteins to leak from the gut into the bloodstream, where our immune systems react against them as invaders and thus the allergic response of runny nose and sneezing.

The entire body is affected by the health of the digestive tract, meaning we should ask the Holy Spirit what it is that we may need in this particular area.

"My mother has a rare form of non-Hodgkin's lymphoma," a woman named Janet Donohue of Sacramento, California, wrote me. "Her oncologist told her five years ago that they could give her no more treatments for her cancer. This was her death sentence. A friend told her about Essiac tea and also asparagus tea. She contacted [a dealer in herbs] and they agreed. Her body is filled with tumors everywhere. The teas keep the tumors shrunken. There have been a couple of times when she could not drink the tea for an extended period of time and the tumors began to grow again. They become visible. After restarting the tea, the tumors shrink again. She has a wonderful quality of life and is doing very well."

Limit your exposure to those things like lawn pesticides, household chemicals, and radiation that may cause "free radicals" to ping around your cells. "Just about everyone I know has someone with cancer in the family, maybe more than one," a doctor from California wrote me. "A major cause not often discussed is electro-motive force (EMF) radiation. A local doctor who treats breast diseases told a nurse that he is seeing more breast cancer in nurses, often in the area where they have a pocket in their scrubs in which they place their cell phones. One pediatrician came out and said that two-year-olds are getting cancer. A friend doc found breast cancer in a nine-year-old. Is it chemicals, yes. Chemo nurses have a high rate of cancer because they are exposed to toxic chemicals at their jobs. Is it our polluted water, especially with hormones? Yes. But the EMF exposure is huge: from computers to cell phones to cordless home phones to TVs and on it goes: So many people have no idea how exposed they are! In hospitals nurses sit in the nurses stations surrounded by many computers. They are exposed all day. How many of our nurses will die from this?"

"I have read with interest your recent articles on cancer," wrote another, Kathy Tylka. "I was diagnosed this past May with pancreatic cancer. My doctors were totally baffled as they claim I don't fit the cancer profile. I do not drink, or smoke, and I eat healthy and exercise and have been healthy all of my sixty-two years. I was a kindergarten teacher for thirty-eight years, loving my job and blessing the children I taught. Why did God allow this disease to enter my body? I have never questioned His reason for He knows better than I what is good for me. My cancer has, in reality, been a blessing. Amazingly wonderful events have taken place because of it. It has lead my four children to a deeper life of prayer, a miracle in itself! People who I barely know have offered many prayers for me. In fact, most days I feel as if I am totally sustained by their prayers. I united my suffering with Jesus on the Cross for all who are battling this horrific disease and He has given me great comfort. My children organized a cancer event they titled the 'Walk of Hope.' The people (including our priest) in my small community (population five thousand) came together and the results were amazing! We raised over $6,000, which we donated to the hospital where I receive treatments. This money will help people who have lost their jobs due to cancer. This fund was actually started by my oncologist, who by the way has told me several times to 'pray always because prayer works better than chemo.'"

Sometimes, there is a purpose. God is such a mystery. Never get angry with He Who allows you to live forever.

We get ill or don't handle the illness in the correct fashion when we stray from His Plan. He guides everyone differently. "The same government that says gay marriage is okay and promiscuity is healthy and must be paid for has also told everyone to eat less fat, but more starch," wrote another from a different perspective. "But the reverse is true. Cut carbs and you will lose weight. Everyone I know (including a friend who reversed their type-2 diabetes) did so by doing exactly the opposite. No sugar, and also no bread, pasta, cereal, or grains (like corn) or starchy vegetables like potatoes. Meat, most cheeses, green vegetables. Since I'm not starving inside, I eat far less, have lost thirty pounds (kept off for three years), have energy, lower blood pressure, and good health. I don't have any cravings for sugar or starch. I was the other way for decades and would fast and work hard but with heroic effort would only lose five pounds that came right back. Sugar and starch cause you to be physically addicted to them."

"I wanted to send a short e-mail about my dad who was cured of prostate cancer that had spread to the bone by changing the way he ate," wrote Barbara Kleaveland. "He had been a daily communicant at his church for almost thirty years and felt that it was the Lord who showed him this way of eating. The diet was called macrobiotics. No animal, fish, dairy, refined sugar, and limited oil. No oil in the beginning. After only three months of eating this way, the cancer began to leave. Eventually he was totally healed of the disease. He died of Alzheimer's at age eighty-five, almost twenty years later. He started a support group for cancer patients and once a month people came and learned how to eat healthy food to boost their immune systems. Recently I watched a documentary on this subject called 'Forks Over Knives.' Many people are becoming aware that our diets can make us sick or make us well. It seems that meat, dairy, and carbs that are made of white flour, white sugar, etcetera and all the excess oils are the culprits. Years ago folks ate a peasant type of food: beans, rice, wheat, barley, and other grains, seeds, nuts, vegetables and fruits.

According to a book I just read called, *My Beef With Meat* by Rip Esselstyn, humans eat over sixty billion animals each year. If we lined the animals up, they would stretch from earth to the moon, two-and-a half times. And we are now learning that calcium pills are not curing weak bones but it is the dairy and meat consumption that causes the calcium to leak from our bones to counteract the acidic condition they cause. Dairy also causes tumor growth due to 'casein,' the animal protein that makes up eighty-six percent of most dairy foods. I do believe we have to change the way we eat, in a drastic way, which totally goes against all that we were taught about healthy eating."

There is Cliff Beckwith, a fellow who, according to *Outsmart Your Cancer*, had stage-four prostate cancer that had spread to his lymph glands. He went on hormonal drugs but augmented that with flaxseed oil mixed in cottage cheese—a sulfurous food that helps to integrate beneficial fats (omega-three and omega-six in the flaxseed).

For two-and-a-half years he mixed two tablespoons of flaxseed oil with half a cup of cottage cheese and crushed pineapples or frozen strawberries for flavor. Initially, he'd had a "PSA" reading of 75—a hormonal indicator of major problems in the prostate. After just six months, however, the doctor's office called in shock: his PSA was down to 0.1 (a completely normal level).

There are cures in nature for things large and small.

I discovered the wonder of tart cherry juice, which is available at the supermarket and gives one a deep restful sleep.

"We are Christians and knew that we needed to seek the Lord's guidance in this crisis," said a woman whose husband had the worst kind of brain cancer, glioblastoma, which is associated with medical radiation, possibly cell phones, and artificial sweeteners. "Tom did not go vegetarian, but we did cut back on meat and sugar. We follow the biblical eating laws and do not eat any pork or unclean fish. It makes it harder for your body to fight cancer if you put unclean and artificial things into it. We think artificial sweetener caused Tom's cancer. He used to drink at least two liters of diet soda a day."

22

Your destiny is the best outcome

'All things are possible to him who believes' (Mark 9:23)

Final outcomes are in the Hands of God.

Seek Him personally everywhere you are and seek Him in the Eucharist, which brings humility.

Humility is closeness to the God of healing.

Seek Him in church near those candles that flicker and "suggest hidden corners."

A daily prayer—"Lord, please fill me with purity and love, purity and love"—can bring miracles. Shout from the heart.

Make it a "desperate" prayer powered by love.

Expect the impossible.

We must never give up hope. You can't experience victory if you plan for defeat. When Jesus was headed for the Cross, He could bear it because His Eyes were on what would come after. There is always glory, when we seek it, when we truly want it, when we plan for it (and thank God before it happens). Don't be the architect of your own failure. Don't draw up a "blackprint" of your future. With Jesus and your angels (ask for extra ones) and the Blessed Mother and the Holy Spirit: all will turn out well in whatever way. Everything is good if we let it be good. Everyone goes through angst, which is a trial of life. We worry about how to pay for our health care. We have debts from a home or a car. We fall back in payments. There's tension at work. We see incredible things on the news. If we allow the devil to discourage us, we fall into lethargy and cast ourselves into the doldrums; we bring a cloud even when there was no cloud. We see all that goes on in society and wonder why anything matters if the world is "going to hell in a hand basket." The answer is to make sure you aren't in that hand basket. *Separate yourself from darkness.* Disappointments must be turned into energy. A disappointment is dead wood to fuel your fire. A "bad report"—a worry—should energize. It does no good to mull over the negative. We lose our spark when we dwell on darkness. The right attitude will take you through any "furnace," through any oppression, to a higher place. The more things are difficult for you, the greater your chance of enhancing His Glory. We all find ourselves on the "threshing floor." That means being refined. Nothing is white, nothing is light, if there is darkness. In Heaven, the Light of Jesus is white. His robe is white. The robes of the saints are white—pure. Black absorbs all the light while white reflects and radiates it. God puts you in situations so you come out higher (and whiter). When we persist, He takes away what has been holding us back. It forms the challenges of earth; pressure brings forth impurities; so does heat. If we respond in the right way, pain or discomfort can prepare us for our destinies. There is the opportunity for more faith and strength. When you can have peace no matter how "bad" the report is, this means progress; the "threshing floor" has turned into your friend. God puts us in situations that purge what keeps us from Him and our missions. Move forward, always forward. If you are focused on what's behind you, you are headed backwards. Often, you have to lose something to gain something. When God takes something away,

He gives more back. It is only separation from God that should concern us when the "going gets rough"; for when the going gets tough, the tough—headed for wellness, healing through God—get on their knees.

Notes

My thanks and much love to my wife, Lisa, who as always has done extraordinary editing and—as always—gave sage advice. I would also like to thank my daughter Elizabeth for her help, and Judy Berlinski: as usual a great editor. Thanks to Pete Massari for his proficient cover and Kathleen Jenkins for her assistance.

As for direct material, the quote on the hemorrhage and the case of asthma are from a website called "About Religion." The quote on the angel in the operating room is from *Evidence of the Afterlife* by Jeffrey Long. Some accounts in this book are from the excellent site, Christian Broadcasting Networking, including the quote from the woman whose son was badly injured in the crash of a bus; the case of Shirley Williams (September 15, 2015) and the story of Chris Carlson. The quote from Father Healey was originally in the *Brooklyn Tablet*. The quote from Sister Briege McKenna is from her book, *Miracles Do Happen*. The story about Aidan is from MaryTV. Tanya Harter Pierce's book is *Outsmart Your Cancer*. Dr. Binzel's was *Alive and Well*. Dr. MacNutt's seminal book is called Healing and is splendid for teachings and examples. The Harvard Medical School studies were reported by Harvard Health Publications in 2014 and 2015. Ty Bollinger's book is *Cancer: Think Outside the Box*. Bernard Ruffin's excellent book, used for account of the miraculous healing of Giovanni Savino's eye, and the saint's own healing, is from *Padre Pio: The True Story*, possibly the best book on this saint. The comments on Alzheimer's and dementia were by a minister named Stacie Spielman in a blog called "Aspects of the Occult." The Radio Maria interview was reproduced by Mary TV.com. The account of the light and also the healing of a short leg is from *The Hidden Child of Medjugorje*, as are the quotes from one of the priests who speaks about the invasion of jealousy, Father Slavko Barbaric, considered saintly; I had the pleasure of once speaking with him at length. Ranelle Wallace's book is *The Burning Within*, and what an account this is! The healings at Lourdes are from a website called "Listverse." A reference on after life was Penny Sartori's book, *The Wisdom of Near-Death Experiences*. The quotes from Dr. James Rouman are from *Orthodox Christian Laity*, August 21, 2015. The account of Juan Diego and his uncle is from *A Woman Clothed with the Sun*, edited by John J. Delaney. The information on Saint André Bessette is from website dedicated to him and Ruffin's book, *The Life of Brother André*. Father McCarthy's book, from which I quote, is *A Compendium of Inner Healing*. The quote from Betty Eadie is from her book, *Embraced by the Light*, a book that some have found controversial, others filled with legitimate inspiration. The quote from the Clarks Summit man was from the *Scranton Times-Tribune*, July 20, 2015. Ian McCormack's account is from *Clinically Dead* by Jenney Sharkey. The account of the English woman from St. Albans with cancer comes from a website of "healing testimonies" from Christian Assemblies International, as does a previous account from New Zealand. The material on how the body eliminates toxins is a paraphrase of a passage in William L. Fischer's *How to Fight Cancer & Win*. My information on coconuts come in part from Bruce Fife's Coconut Cures, including the account of Julie. *The China Study* by T. Colin Campbell was the most valuable reference for nutrition. I highly recommend everyone read it! My thanks to all.

Other Books by Michael H. Brown

Available at www.spiritdaily.com

THE SPIRITS AROUND US

LIFE MISSIONS, FAMILY HEALING

THE OTHER SIDE

THE GOD OF MIRACLES

AFTER LIFE

PRAYER OF THE WARRIORS

THE FINAL HOUR

WHAT YOU TAKE TO HEAVEN